ONE to ANOTHER

Preserving
Our Stories
and
Our Land

Marcia Patteson Beckett

Thanks for reading!
Marcia Beckett

Printed by Puritan Press, Inc., Hollis, NH

Contents

Introduction

This book grew out of a chance meeting with Marion Lull Howe on Halloween night back in 2002. I was out trick-or-treating with my husband, our three children and some friends when we knocked on Marion's door to get what we expected would be the usual doling out of candy. Well, come to find out, Marion's idea of Halloween had more to do with people than it did candy.

She opened her door wide for us to come in for a neighborly visit, introducing us to her handicapped adult son Stephen, who sat in his wheelchair parked next to the couch. He, like his mother, considered Halloween the perfect excuse to socialize. Flaunting a giant pair of bright green sunglasses he invited the kids to help themselves to the candy-filled plastic pumpkin sitting on the couch. The kids, disguised in their frog, cheerleader, Dracula and grass-skirt-glamour-girl costumes, indulged in their sweet treats while Marion got out a photo album to show us some old photographs of Hollis. Although I recognized where the pictures had been taken, they were definitely from a different time. They were from a time unhurried when plowing an acre a day with a horse-drawn plow was a good day's work. It was a time that obviously intrigued me because not only did I listen to Marion that night, I returned about a dozen times to hear more. I went back again and again to hear Marion's stories because I liked the tempo of time she knew when life was slower and people lived off the land.

As my husband and I looked at Marion's album, peripherally aware of the kids' amazing patience, I experienced an I-am-my-mother's-daughter moment when you suddenly realize that you are doing exactly what you never thought you would. Growing up, I remember all too frequently my mother befriending complete strangers wherever we went. At the grocery store she'd say to the cashier, "What a lovely dress you're wearing." At a restaurant she would have some nice comment to say to our waitress such as, "You're a nice person." I usually smiled, being a good sport, though more times than not I really just wanted to either hide or prod my mother along. Nevertheless, I always did as my children did that night in Marion's living room. I waited ever so patiently for her to finish. I know I'll never go as far as my mother did inviting the lunchtime wait staff from the Four Seasons in Boston over to our house to play croquet or asking the nice widower from church over for Thanksgiving dinner, but I do find myself listening to people's stories.

My visits with Marion took on a simple pattern. I'd call her to ask when I could come over and she'd say, "Oh anytime is okay with me. Sometimes I go with my daughter, Sharon, to take Stephen to the doctor, but other than that I am home." So, with an agreed upon day and time, I'd arrive at her house with my notebook and pen in hand, knocking on her white, wide panel door with its little black, wrought iron latch, enjoying time as a country journalist.

Surprisingly, at 92 years old, Marion was not a shuffler. She had as much intent as she did integrity, with a kind of quiet flair that held me somewhat on the edge of my seat. In my mind, Marion was a woman of her own making. She had a get-up-and-go, ride-that-motorcycle attitude I admire. Standing about five feet tall with bright blue eyes, gray hair and a smiling face that sparkled I couldn't help but be drawn in.

Each time I visited we sat at her kitchen table that, she made a point to tell me, her husband Clarence had given her on their wedding day back in 1940. Running my hand along its edge, I was struck by its smoothness. I knew such smoothness could only come from years of use and more than that, from years of memories in the making. It was a table that held a rich history, which now I too would become part as Marion and I shared a bit of life while her son, Stephen, sat in his wheelchair at her side.

Our visits continued over the next several years until Marion died unexpectedly in 2006. When I last called Marion to meet, she told me she couldn't because Stephen was in the hospital. Ironically, amid Stephen's illness, Marion developed stomach pain, and unfortunately died of a heart attack just days before he came home from the hospital. I could not believe this smiling, steadfast woman was gone and our visits were over.

The last thing Marion said to me was, "Hold onto that book." After I told her I would, I hung up the phone feeling as if she knew something I didn't. I had this pervasive, sinking feeling that I would not be seeing her again. Her words felt prematurely final. It seemed as if, somehow, she had an inkling that she was going to die.

Marion's older sister Hilda Hildreth, who at the time was 99, called me a few weeks after Marion died to give me the news, but more than that, to tell me she wanted to help finish what Marion and I had begun. Upon meeting Hilda for the first time she told me how strange it was not talking with Marion anymore. Every night at 6 o'clock Marion had called Hilda to talk. She even called the night before she died. Hilda, looking at her phone sitting on the table in front of her chair, said, "My phone doesn't even ring. I suppose I don't really need it anymore."

This book came to be because after I met with Marion a couple of times I had a strong sense that her story could be appreciated beyond her kitchen. I saw value in knowing more about a way of life far removed from the abundance of things today. I asked Marion if she would mind if I wrote a book telling of her family's farming days gone by. She was thrilled. And, now I am glad to say that I have in fact "held onto this book." I have brought it to fruition as I intended to do; for myself and for Marion.

So, that Halloween night back in 2002 was the beginning—the beginning of a story about Marion's family starting Lull Farm in Hollis, New Hampshire, back in 1918. It was the beginning of a story worth sharing simply because it is from a time when farming truly was a way of life and people were connected by the common thread of their stories.

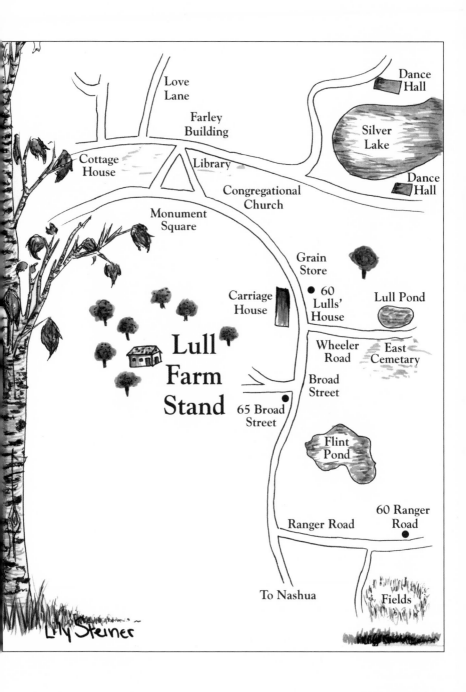

Love
Lane

Farley
Building

Dance
Hall

Silver
Lake

Cottage
House

Library

Congregational
Church

Dance
Hall

Monument
Square

Grain
Store

Lull Pond

Carriage
House

● 60
Lulls'
House

Wheeler
Road

East
Cemetary

Lull
Farm
Stand

Broad
Street

65 Broad
Street

Flint
Pond

60 Ranger
Road

Ranger Road

To Nashua

Fields

Lily Steiner

The Lull Family

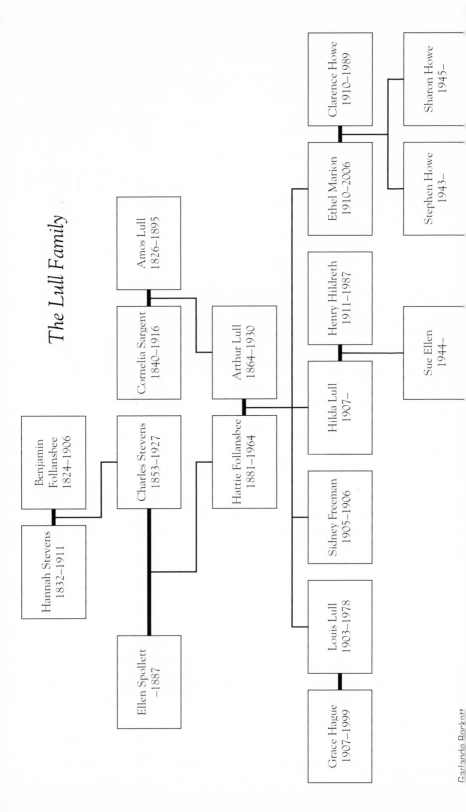

Benjamin Follansbee 1824–1906

Hannah Stevens 1832–1911

Amos Lull 1826–1895

Cornelia Sargent 1840–1916

Charles Stevens 1853–1927

Ellen Spollett –1887

Arthur Lull 1864–1930

Hattie Follansbee 1881–1964

Louis Lull 1903–1978

Grace Hague 1907–1999

Sidney Freeman 1905–1906

Hilda Lull 1907–

Henry Hildreth 1911–1987

Sue Ellen 1944–

Ethel Marion 1910–2006

Clarence Howe 1910–1989

Stephen Howe 1943–

Sharon Howe 1945–

CHAPTER I

Arthur Lull

Arthur had no intention of becoming a farmer like his father, yet, as is often the case, things did not turn out the way he envisioned. Growing up on the same farm as his father on Lull Road in New Boston, New Hampshire, Arthur wanted to experience life beyond farming. In his mid-twenties he packed up and left home to partner with his cousin who owned a grocery store in Providence, Rhode Island. Arthur's girlfriend, Etheleila, who apparently wasn't worth staying home for, was more than disappointed when the man she had her heart set on moved away to create a life for himself far different from what he knew or others expected.

Arthur quickly established himself as a grocer, enjoying his self-sufficient life in the city until, just a couple of years into the business, Arthur's father Amos died, leaving his mother Cornelia alone on their farm in New Boston. Being the good man that he was, Arthur felt he had no choice but to return home to help his mother. So, he headed back to New Boston, hanging up his suit to put on overalls, picking up farming where his father left off. In his quiet, determinied way, he managed the hens, sold eggs house-to-house from New Boston to Manchester, grew vegetables for the farmers' market in Manchester and did carpentry work wherever he could. Arthur worked hard seven days a week, from dawn to well past dusk, doing whatever it took to support himself and his mother.

The one enjoyment he looked forward to each week was hitching up his horse and carriage to go to the prayer meeting at the Union Church in Weare, six miles away. Those meetings proved to be a good thing because a woman by the name of Hattie Follansbee who was the church organist had something Etheleila clearly didn't. When Arthur saw Hattie playing the organ, sitting up tall, wrapped in her music, he must have had one of those rare but magical moments when you know someone is going to be part of your life.

Hattie Follansbee had smooth, light skin with blue-sky, attentive eyes. Her waves of brown hair sat easily around her

The Lull Family

Front Row: Hattie Follansbee Lull (Marion's mother) holding Happy, Marion Lull, Cousin Edna, Hilda Lull (Marion's older sister)

Back Row: "Big Edna" Follansbee (Hattie's stepmother), Louis Lull (Marion's brother), Charles Follansbee (Hattie's father), Arthur Lull (Marion's father)

face with the rest pinned back in a loose bun at the nape of her neck.

Hattie's hair reminds me of my own mother who also had a bun, though my mother didn't pin hers up loosely. That's not my mother's style. She was much more formal than that. My mother's bun required a ritual of assembly I remember vividly. As a young girl I often sat on my mother's king-sized bed to watch her expert bunning skill. Standing in front of her dressing mirror, she'd bend over, hanging her head at her knees to first brush her shoulder length, almost black, thin hair, saying "Always brush 100 times." I never counted her brush strokes and I'm pretty sure she never did either. Nevertheless, her hair got brushed. Still bent over, she twisted her hair tightly into a circle at the back of her head pinning it up, making an "x" with two bobby pins. With her mini-bun in place she then got her 18" long, thick, braided hairpiece of the same color to wind around the mini-bun.

Curious about the hairpiece, I once asked my mother where she got it. She told me it was her own hair that she had had cut years before. I never questioned it then, but looking back I don't think it was my mother's hair. She didn't have thick hair.

Over the years, my three older brothers and I have come to realize as adults that my mother seemed to have had a somewhat casual relationship with the truth. My mother told us that my uncle was buried at Arlington Cemetery. Well, either my uncle changed his name or he isn't buried at Arlington. No harm done. My uncle is I-don't-know-where and my mother's hair is I-don't-know-whose, but in the grand scheme of things it really doesn't matter.

Arthur and Hattie fell in love and were married on May 21, 1902. He was thirty-seven, she was twenty-one. While their age difference might have raised some eyebrows, their ages never got in the way. They were a team. They worked incredibly hard to support themselves and their growing family.

I think of my own mother who, as a single parent, worked hard for our family of five. My father died of cancer when I was six months old. My brothers were nine, six and four. My mom was thirty-six.

My mother didn't have a job when my father died so she made ends meet by selling revolutionary unbreakable dishware and making beeswax candles. I remember each week a different group of ladies assembled in our living room to listen to my mother's spiel about the incredible unbreakable plates. Then, in what felt to me like an edge-of-your-seat demonstration I'd come in all dressed up in an ironed dress, white lace-trimmed ankle socks and black patent-leather shoes to stand on a plate. Voila, mission accomplished.

Starting Out

Hattie didn't sell plates. Neither did Arthur, but they, like everyone else, did whatever it took to make a precious dollar. After Hattie and Arthur married they lived with his mother, Cornelia, at their small family farm on Lull Road in New Boston. For the most part, the threesome worked out well with Hattie following Cornelia's lead, manning the house while Arthur did the farm work. After a year under the same roof, Cornelia decided it was time to move on. She wanted to move closer to her mother and two sisters who

Arthur and Hattie's farm in New Boston, New Hampshire

lived in Goffstown, while giving Arthur and Hattie the chance to start a life of their own. Telling Arthur and Hattie her plans, they soon prepared to sell the farm.

Cornelia bought a spacious, rather stately white Georgian (The Governor Morrill's House) in Grasmere, which was a small hamlet of Goffstown. For her, the move marked a new beginning in that she would be on her own for the first time in her life.

Hattie and Arthur found an old farmhouse in New Boston at the foot of the Uncanoonuc Mountains. Scraping up all the money they could and borrowing the rest, they bought the farmhouse with attached shed and barn on fifteen acres of land for $700.

They moved into their first home in early 1903. This would be the home where their four children would be born. Their first child, Louis, was born in 1904 in Weare at Hattie's grandmother's house where, most likely, a neighbor or doctor came to help with the birth. Their second child, Sidney, born in 1905, tragically died after falling out of bed before

Halley's Comet as it appeared over Flagstaff, Arizona, on May 13, 1910. The streaks at lower left are the city lights of Flagstaff, and the large bright object below the comet is the planet Venus. The best known of all comets, Halley orbits the Sun and travels close enough to the Earth to be seen once every 75 years.[1]

his first birthday. Their third child, Hilda, was born in 1907 at Cornelia's house in Grasmere and their fourth child, E. Marion, was born in 1910 at the hospital in Manchester.

E. Marion was coincidentally born on her parents' eighth wedding anniversary, on a day when the sky happened to be getting quite a bit of attention. After seventy-five years Halley's Comet once again appeared in the sky for all to see. But Halley was not your typical fly-by-night comet. She stuck around for a week, making it hard for anyone to miss. After E. Marion was born, Hattie held her new baby girl up to the window to see the once-in-a-lifetime comet. (Seventy-five years later, E. Marion would have the rare twice-in-a-lifetime privilege of seeing Halley's Comet once again as she looked to the sky.)

What's in a Name?

There's a bit of story behind the "E" in E. Marion's name that is worth explaining. Just before Arthur and Hattie were to have their first child, Cornelia told Arthur that she was going to put $100 in the Manchester Bank for each of her grand-children. She planned the deposit such that each grandchild would receive the money, with the accumulated interest, when each turned twenty-one. There was just one sticky stip-ulation—Cornelia would gain the privilege of naming each of her grandchildren.

Arthur, amazed by the bitter sweetness of his mother's proposal, felt trapped. Although he and Hattie could not imagine relinquishing the naming of their own children, they also couldn't imagine foregoing such a generous gift. Money was hard to come by. So much so, that Cornelia got her wish.

She named Arthur and Hattie's first child Louis, their second child, who died as a baby, Sidney, their third child Hilda, and their fourth child, whose name neither Arthur nor Hattie would have ever chosen, Ethel Marion. Ethel was a shortened version of Etheleila, the name of Arthur's girl-friend before he married Hattie. Cornelia took a sincere lik-ing to Etheleila, hoping very much Arthur would marry her. In the end, although Arthur never married Etheleila, Cor-nelia ingeniously wiggled a bit of that girlfriend into the fam-ily by attempting to name Arthur and Hattie's second daughter after her. Cornelia originally wished to name E. Marion, Etheleila Ardella, after Arthur's girlfriend, but Hat-tie did everything she could do to squash that. Hattie hoped Cornelia would compromise at Ethel Marion Lull. It had a bit of Etheleila as well as a name that Hattie had always

liked. Mercifully, Cornelia agreed. They named their new
baby girl Ethel Marion, which was a lot easier to say and a
whole lot easier to live with.

When Hattie saw Ethel Marion for the first time she
knew the name Ethel would never cross her lips; she would
be known as Marion or more formally, E. Marion Lull.

CHAPTER 2

Marion on a Mission

Bottle Ants

During the spring and summer, the Lulls spent most of their time outside. Hattie worked in the garden, Arthur did carpentry work, Louis went to school or helped his father and Hilda usually played with Marion, keeping an eye on her.

At a year old, Marion had two bottles she drank milk from. She treasured her bottles, made of thick glass with a black rubber nipple, oftentimes bringing one outside with her while Hattie worked in the garden. Marion traipsed around drinking her bottle with her head tilted back just enough to suck the fresh cow milk from the nipple until it was gone. Coveting her bottle, she would then discreetly hide it under the lilac bush, next to the house, for safe keeping. Hours later Hattie would find Marion's bottle in her secret hiding place with a mass of ants eating away at the nipple. The next time Marion did this was the last. Hattie rightly figured that if she was clever enough to hide her bottles, then she was clever enough to drink from a cup.

Pa's Tools

When Marion was four years old she acted on an idea she thought rather entertaining, much to her father's chagrin. She went out the kitchen door, along the attached shed, which

From the left: Hilda, Marion with her bottle, and Hattie ("Ma")

was an enclosed, elongated walkway from the house to the barn, to get some of Arthur's, or as she called him, "Pa's," tools. She then walked back through the shed to the privy (the family "toilet") inside the kitchen end of the shed, to perform a little experiment. She wanted to know what it would sound like when she dropped each of Pa's tools down the hole of the privy bench into the freshly thawed waste below.

While you can imagine the sound, you can also probably imagine Arthur's expression when he went to the barn for his tools only to learn from Marion where they were. But being the good man that Arthur was, he stoically retrieved his tools from the privy, cleaned them off and knew without having to say a word that it would not happen again.

When I think of a time that I wish I could rewind the minutes, as Marion probably did when her father went looking for his tools, the first thing that comes to mind is when I was about eight years old helping my brothers paint our front porch. I had the tedious job of painting the balusters of the front railing. Sitting there painting one after another, it is no surprise that I ended up with white bangs, but fortunately I had the perfect solution. I went upstairs to get some scissors and cut my bangs up to my hairline. Well, I did do a great job getting rid of my painted hair, though I also succeeded in giving myself a frontal crew cut. The thought of going to school was all the humiliation I needed to stay away from scissors for a long time. Just like Marion, I never did that again.

Winter Hardship

Winters were a daily battle against the cold. In a fervent effort to stay warm Arthur cut all the wood he could from the trees they had on their property to use in what were their only sources of heat—the parlor stove and the cook stove. While the stoves put out the heat they needed to make it through the crisp days of November, the biting cold of December forced them out of the house to move in with Arthur's mother in Grasmere. Although they would still be cold there, it was warm enough to live out the rest of the winter.

Before temporarily moving to Cornelia's, Louis and Hilda attended a one-room schoolhouse, walking two miles each way while Marion, too young yet for school, stayed home with her mother helping her make bread, cook and wash the clothes in large tin buckets. On snowy days Arthur drove Louis and Hilda to school in the horse wagon that had runners to slice through the snow.

In addition to the difficulty of staying warm, Arthur and Hattie did whatever they could to earn money to supplement the meager supply of food they had from their garden. Every winter Arthur scoured the woods for laurel that Hattie made into roping and wreaths to sell in Manchester during the holidays. Wealthy city people took pride in decorating their homes with the lovely greenery for the Christmas season. They strung laurel swags along a fence, they festooned their front door and they hung wreaths. The more they decorated the better Arthur and Hattie could keep serious cold and hunger at bay.

Hattie made roping by breaking stem after stem of laurel into ten inch long pieces she then gathered into bunches to wrap tightly with thin wire. Marion liked helping her mother. The only bad part was seeing her mother's hands crack and bleed from working with the wire in the cold, dry air. But Hattie did not let pain get in the way. She just worked without pause, making lengths of roping until the laurel was gone.

We never made laurel swags, but we did make beeswax candles to sell at our church fair. There we would be on a Sunday afternoon, my mom, my three brothers and I sitting at our dining room table in an assembly line making dozens of candles. My mother heated each sheet of wax on a little portable, two burner, coil stove until it was pliable enough to roll. Then we'd lay the warmed beeswax sheets on waxed paper where we'd place a long wick at one edge before rolling it up into a candle. Once the candles were made we bundled them in groups of six, tying them with a satin ribbon.

Freestones

In the evening the Lulls stayed warm by huddling around their parlor stove playing Old Maid or reading a story, from their treasured box of books, by the light of the kerosene lantern hanging from the ceiling. While the family enjoyed time together in the parlor their freestones heated on the cook stove to get toasty warm before going to bed. Wrapping the hot freestones in an old flannel cloth or newspaper, Hattie gave them each one to bring to bed. Marion cherished her freestone bed warmer because she knew it made all the difference between a good night's sleep and one that brought little, if any, sleep. The freestones, made of gray soapstone blocks, cut about two inches thick, six inches wide and eight inches long with a curved wire handle at the top for carrying, were an important part of winter.

Moving to Cornelia's

When the water in the wash bowls began to freeze it was time to move to Cornelia's, or as Marion knew her, Grandmother Lull's, for the winter. The move entailed packing the few belongings they owned, hitching the horse to the wagon and driving seven miles to Grasmere. Marion didn't mind staying with her Grandmother Lull although she could be a bit of a scrooge with a definite, determined way of doing things.

At night, the Lulls enjoyed time together in the parlor reading, playing card games or listening to Hattie tell stories. Oftentimes they sat in the dark because Grandmother Lull refused to light the lamp. She didn't want to waste the kerosene. For her, sitting in the dark clearly made more sense than using kerosene. So, there they'd be all huddled around the woodstove with only the blue light of the moon shining through the windows as they listened intently to Hattie tell stories about days gone by while the wind chased the snow outside.

Brown Sugar Hair

Grandmother Lull liked everything to be in order—her house, her clothes and anything else that could be organized. She even took it upon herself to ensure Marion and Hilda's hair was tidy. Every morning she brushed their hair, tugging through tangles with uncompromising determination before rewarding them with an ingenious concoction of brown sugar mixed with a trickle of water to keep their bangs in place. Grandmother Lull's sticky, gooey paste worked wonders, as far as she was concerned. Marion's hair had no way of even

Hilda and Marion

thinking about going astray; it was glued to the sides of her face.

Marion would have actually liked to use some of her grandmother's glue on her Aunt Alice who had a couple long, black, wiry hairs protruding prominently from her chin. Taming those hairs would have been a good thing. Each time Marion had to kiss her aunt on the cheek she cringed at the thought of those tickling hairs. What she would have done for a bit of brown sugar goo.

Never Again

August 6, 1916 marked the day that Marion would begin missing her Grandmother Lull. She would miss her frugality and even her brown sugar solutions because now she was gone. Soon after Grandmother Lull died, a man they did not know came to their house in New Boston to tell Arthur of his mother's passing. Without hesitation, Arthur hitched up the horse and wagon for them to go to Grasmere to pay their respects. There they would see Grandmother Lull laid out in the front parlor of her house to see her one last time before being buried.

Cornelia Lull

Many years later, at age ninety-two, Marion could recall with vivid clarity the details of this experience. She remembered the prominent black wreath made of wide, shiny taffeta ribbon hanging on the front door to show that Cornelia Lull had died. She remembered her Grandmother dressed in black as if going to her own funeral, wearing a long black dress, black stockings and black dress shoes.

These images stayed with Marion for the rest of her life such that she made it clear to her own two children, Sharon and Stephen, never to lay her out like that when her time came. She did not want anyone to experience what she had on that dark day back in 1916.

On Stage

Hattie must have seen early on Marion's ability to entertain because when Marion was just six years old Hattie encouraged her to memorize a poem to recite at the New Boston Town Hall before an audience. A little encouragement was all Marion needed. She no sooner memorized the poem her mother had given her successfully taking it to the stage, marking what would be the first of many performances.

My Garden
By Suzanne Weddell
(Performed by Marion Lull, 1916)

My papa makes pretty flowers grow
By digging holes in the ground, down low,
And dropping in seeds –
So many he needs –
And pretty soon flowers stand there in a row.
I wanted a garden like papa's too.
'Twas down in my sand-pile, and I thought
'twould do.
To plant my dear dolly,
Because 'twould be jolly
To have lots of dollies, all pretty and new.
So I planted, and watered her well every day,
But she just wouldn't grow in the flowers' good way.
She stayed in the ground,

And I never found
A single new dolly growing up to play.
My papa says dollies don't grow any more,
But stay just the way they come out of the store.
So I guess 'twould be better
To go out and get her
And have my dear dolly, the same as before.

Dragonfly Tears

Marion started school in New Boston when she was six years old. She ventured out every morning with Louis and Hilda for their long, two mile trek to school. Two miles was a long way for Louis and Hilda and just too plain long for Marion's six-year-old legs.

On one particular morning, Marion found herself lagging behind farther than usual. Reaching the creek bridge just a few minutes from home, a silent dragonfly with its diaphanous wings came darting at her out of nowhere. Marion tried to swoosh it away, but it kept at her. She knew she couldn't catch up to Louis and Hilda so she ran home, trying to see through the dragonfly tears that filled her eyes. Bursting in the kitchen door Hattie immediately comforted Marion, listening to what had happened. As Marion told her mother everything about that awful dragonfly her fears spilled into the warmth and safety of her mother's arms.

Marion did not go to school the next day because she had an awful tummy ache and she didn't go the day after that either. In fact, she didn't go back for the rest of the year. Instead, as soon as Hattie told Marion that she didn't have to go to school for the rest of the year Marion's tummy aches miraculously disappeared. From the dragonfly day on, Marion shadowed her mother. She sat on the flour barrel watching her knead bread dough, she helped her roll out pie pastry and she lent a hand scrubbing the clothes. Marion got a great education that year. While she learned a bit about self-sufficiency, she learned a lot about being loved.

Blueberry Tears

One day, the last week in July, when the blueberries were perfectly ripe, Marion went blueberry picking with her family. Arthur had gotten permission from a man who lived a few miles away to pick blueberries on his property. Preparing for a hot summer day of picking, Hattie packed lunch and collected their picking baskets while Arthur filled a bucket with water for the horse.

Upon arriving, after tying the horse to a tree, they fastened their baskets around their waist freeing both hands for productive picking. The race was on. As much as Marion and Hilda loved picking, the heat of the sun cramped their stamina. Unlike Arthur, Hattie and Louis who could go nonstop, the girls needed periodic breaks to cool down in the shade of tree.

At the end of the day, before leaving for home Hattie looked in each basket to relish the joy of their blueberry harvest. Looking into Marion's basket she saw the berries littered with pieces of twine from the rope around Marion's waist. Her berries couldn't be used. As Marion watched her mother dump all the blueberries that she had worked so hard to pick, under a bush tears filled her eyes. Big fat blueberry tears.

At about the same age Marion was in her blueberry story, I too had a day of bad luck. Not blueberry bad luck, gasoline bad luck.

It happened the day my brother was mowing the grass. I eyed a green Ginger Ale bottle standing upright on the curb at the edge of the lawn. It was a hot summer day so when I saw the thirst quenching Ginger Ale I thought I'd steal a sip when he wasn't looking. I don't remember anything past picking up the green bottle and bringing it to my mouth. My mother called the doctor who told her to give me a lot of milk to drink and that I should rest. Well, I definitely rested; I think I worked on sleeping that sip off for the rest of the day plus some.

Come to find out, there was gasoline in the soda bottle because my brother couldn't carry the heavy gas can from the garage to the mower when it ran out of gas. So, he had the "clever" idea to pour some into an empty soda bottle to keep nearby if he needed it. Well, I don't know if he needed it, but I do know that I did not.

Lightning Fires

Marion, like most people during these times, had an understandable fear of thunderstorms because lightening sometimes resulted in disaster. Lightening had the unforgiving potential to burn homes or barns to the ground, invariably ruining a family's entire livelihood in a single storm. New Boston, like most rural farming towns, did not have any fire wagons or trucks so as a building burned there was no stopping it. Spreading flames devoured barns as well as the animals inside. Cows perished because they were lined up side-by-side confined in their stanchions. Stabled horses could sometimes break free from their stalls, in the wild terror of a fire, though more times than not the flames engulfed them as well. The sheep enclosed in pens also burned whereas the chickens were the luckiest of all, they roamed freely.

Once a home or barn burned to the ground there was little a family could do to recover their loss. Although home and business insurance was available, in farming communities like New Boston or Hollis, most people could not afford the luxury of protecting their assets. The animals were the 'tools' of a farm so when they died, the farm did too.

During one particular storm Marion was in the old house in New Boston looking out the kitchen window at the hills in the distance where she spotted six or seven barn roofs on fire. The lightening fires instilled in her a dread of storms from that day on.

Shingles

One Sunday afternoon a man came running to the Lulls' house hollering to Arthur that there was a fire about a half mile away in the woods behind their house. Arthur ran to the barn to grab his shovel before rushing to the woods with the man. Returning home several hours later, Arthur's hair and clothes were damp with sweat. He had a raging fever.

The doctor came the next day to discover that Arthur had shingles. He would need to stay in bed. He ended up sick in bed for two weeks preventing him from going to the store for much needed food. Hattie would have hitched up the horse and wagon, but because she had never done it Arthur was adamant that she not go. The risk was too great. It also wasn't feasible for Louis to make the trip as he was too young to take on that task.

A few days into Arthur's illness, the Lulls ran out of food. They had had a dry summer, drying all the vegetables in their garden and as a result, had nothing stored in the cellar to eat. In a hunger none of them had ever known, Hattie had no choice but to gather her courage to kill one of their hens—a job that Arthur had always done, Hattie was now faced with having to do the ugly deed. Unfortunately, the hen provided little sustenance so Hattie told Louis to go to the nearest neighbor, the Christys, to ask them if they could spare some food. The Christys gave Louis a bottle of milk along with some canned vegetables, which they rationed carefully until Arthur felt well enough to finally go to the store.

I cannot imagine being truly hungry. I have never experienced it, even remotely. Not only have I never been hungry, I've always had the luxury of choices. And oftentimes, so many choices that deciding what to eat posed the only challenge. For breakfast alone, I grew up having the usual choice of Frosted Flakes, Captain Crunch, Lucky Charms (on a good day), Quaker oatmeal, pancakes, eggs or toast. Our kitchen cabinets, refrigerator and hefty freezer in the basement never went without and neither did we.

CHAPTER 3

Lull Farm

New Boston to Hollis

Arthur and Hattie probably would not have made the decision to move from their New Boston home of fifteen years had it not been for two contributing factors. First, Arthur received jury duty notice from the Nashua Courthouse that he was obligated to serve in the upcoming weeks. To do this, he would have to travel twenty-two miles by horse to and from Nashua. It wasn't feasible. He would have to be on his way before dawn to arrive at the Nashua Courthouse on time each morning. Getting home would be no easier.

The other issue concerned life at the foot of the Uncanoonuc Mountains. Here, the growing season, cut short by early frosts and longer winters, made it difficult for them to sustain themselves or make a living. Arthur's jury duty notice served as a blessing in disguise. It gave the Lulls just the momentum they needed to move.

Arthur and Hattie wanted to move closer to Nashua where the population had better potential of supporting their livelihood. They contacted a realtor who told them of three farms for sale in Hollis. The Lulls didn't know much about Hollis, other than it being an established farming community west of Nashua, nonetheless the idea of moving energized them.

In 1918 when the Lulls moved, Hollis's population was roughly 825. Interestingly, the number of people far dwarfed the number of animals. As in most, if not all farming communities, Hollis, like New Boston, had far more animals than it did people simply because animals were the lifeblood of farms in two essential ways—those raised for food or those used for work. New Boston's animal census came in at 4,210 with 2,530 fowl (mostly chickens), 847 cows, 300 horses, 259 hogs, 139 sheep, 117 neat stock (cattle), 16 oxen and 2 mules. Hollis in comparison had a total of 5,850 animals with 4,732 fowl, 613 cows, 313 horses, 67 hogs, 16 sheep, 106 neat stock (cattle), 2 oxen and 1 mule.

The Lulls knew they were in for a little indulgence when the real estate man arrived at their house in New Boston driving a car to pick them up. That in itself was quite a novelty. Upon arriving in Hollis, Marion was pleasantly surprised by how close the houses were to one another. The thought of having a friend live so close that you could run to their house made leaving New Boston all the more inviting.

The first place they visited was the Monroe Hurd Farm, which had been a dairy operation for many years until Mr. Hurd decided to sell the cows and later the farm for reasons unknown. The farm covered about fifty acres in all. Nearly thirty acres on the north side of Broad Street with twenty acres on the south side. The north side of the farm included a one and a half story white clapboard house with its attached shed and barn, two horses and a cow pasture that extended from behind the house to Wheeler Road. The pasture also had a shallow pond that Mr. Hurd had dug for his cows.

The south side of the farm had an ice house attached to a carriage barn, some farm machinery, three apple trees, two plum trees and a pear tree. The price of the farm was $6,000.

After the Lulls toured the Munroe Hurd Farm they went on to see the other two farms nearby. Both of these farms were considerably smaller with much less to offer, making the Munroe Hurd Farm their obvious first choice. The only problem was, could they afford it? After seeing the three farms Arthur told the realtor that he very much wanted to buy the Munroe Hurd Farm, but he would first need to obtain a loan.

Borrowing Money

Arthur succeeded in getting a mortgage from an individual lender in Nashua named Eva Farmer. With a name like that the stars must have been aligned because Ms. Farmer agreed to loan Arthur the entire $6,000 on the condition he pay her $70 four times a year until the loan plus the interest was paid off, which would be sometime in the early 1940s. The obligation of this long-term debt did not seem to concern Arthur. For the first time in his life he would have a farm of his own to develop as he wished. He felt confident that he had the ability to farm as well as any other farmer in Hollis to make a comfortable living. He would pay back the loan, but first he and his family would start anew.

Bicycle Marathon

As the Lulls prepared to move, Arthur asked Mr. Hurd if he could borrow his team of horses and wagon enabling them to make the move from New Boston to Hollis in one trip rather than several. Mr. Hurd generously agreed. But it wasn't

Louis Lull

Arthur who went to get the horse and wagon, it was Louis. It was time for Louis at fifteen to try on more responsibility so Arthur asked his son to ride his bicycle twenty miles to get Mr. Hurd's wagon and horses to bring back to New Boston. For Louis to ride his bicycle all that way alone over rocky dirt roads, on a trip that he had made only once before required all the bravado he, and his mother for that matter, could muster. While Louis was gone, Hattie half held her breath until late that afternoon when, finally hearing the jingle of the horses' harnesses coming up the hill, she could finally free the worry that filled her.

I had a similar, although circuitous, experience of accomplishment when I was about twelve years old. Having the day off from school, my mother, who worked at the Joslin-Diabetes Foundation in Boston, thought it would be nice for me to take the trolley by myself into town to meet her for lunch and go clothes shopping. I jumped at the chance to go shopping for the simple reason that my mother was generally not a shopper, although interestingly she owned more shoes than anyone I knew. Her shoes were arranged in their very own compact closet of shelves where numerous boxes were labeled and stacked.

My assignment was to take the trolley from the Newton Riverside station, near our house, to the "Longwood" stop where she would wait for me. Easy enough. I got on the trolley with my quarters in hand dropping them into the coin collector as if I did it every day. After several stops we came to "Longwood Towers" where I immediately thought I should get off, but certain that my mother told me to get off at "Longwood," I figured it was probably the next stop. As we proceeded underground, which I knew "Longwood" was not, I thought "Oh, oh."

As I saw everyone around me as calm as could be I didn't know what to do. Standing up from my seat, trying not to land in someone's lap I held onto whatever I could, managing my way forward to ask the driver where "Longwood" was. He told me it was the previous stop. I should have gotten off at "Longwood Towers." Great. Now what? At the next stop the driver stepped off the train extending his hand to me to help me across the tracks to the other side. He told me to get on the next trolley getting off at "Longwood Towers." I did just as he said. The moment I saw my mother standing next to the "Longwood Towers" sign, perplexed as to why I was coming from the opposite direction, relief filled me. Just as it must have filled Louis and Hattie when he made it home.

Auction

With the addition of Mr. Hurd's wagon the Lulls intended to make their move in a single trip. The only thing they needed to do was sell some of their belongings. Arthur and Hattie hired an auctioneer to come to their house to sell what they could. On the day of the auction the Lulls were impressed by the number of empty wagons that arrived at their house ready to take their things away. With a good number of people there by early morning the auctioneer got right to it, calling out bids selling item after item like a race to the finish.

The next day Hattie, Marion and Hilda piled all that was left—their linens, dishes, utensils and pots and pans—into wooden crates while Arthur and Louis moved the heavy dressers, beds, mirrors and tools. After the wagons were loaded they got one last thing—their dining room table, which they stood upright over the crates on one wagon. With the wagons ready to go, they settled in for their last night in New Boston.

Early the next morning after what must have been a restless night's sleep for the Lulls in anticipation of their new life in Hollis, Arthur and Louis prepared the four horses for the trip. While the men fed and watered the horses the girls

Auction in New Boston

searched for Hilda's missing black and white cat she aptly named Puppy. Pressed for time, wanting to reach Hollis before dark, they unfortunately had to get on their way without ever finding Puppy.

Arthur drove one wagon with Hilda up front next to him while Louis drove the other wagon sitting next to Hattie. Marion had the most memorable seat of all. She sat on top of the dining room table holding Puppy's new kittens in a basket on her lap.

Although Hattie expected to make most if not the whole trip sitting next to Louis, she had no such luck. Their stodgy cow needed prodding so Hattie had to walk behind it for the better part of the trip, switching it with a long, thin flexible stick to swat at its rear end to keep it moving. That cow proved to be more work than it was probably worth, though it did provide them with milk. It did not take long for Hattie's feet to become blistered and swollen from walking for miles in what were the only shoes she owned. The ankle cut, lace up dress boots with a two and half inch stocky heel, which were hand-me-downs from her sister who worked at the shoe factory in Manchester, were not only one size too small, but were also not meant for hours of walking. They made for an agonizing trip to Hollis.

After walking about ten miles, arriving in Amherst, their old cow refused to budge. It just stood there in the middle of the road as if stuck in place. Arthur went to the nearest house to ask the woman who lived there if she would allow them to leave their cow in her back pasture until they came back for it later. The woman graciously agreed. The only problem now was getting the stubborn cow to move. After consistent

The Lulls' farm, 60 Broad Street, Hollis, New Hampshire, 1918
This is looking from the south side of the Lulls' farm across Broad Street to the house and barn on the north side. The white barn was torn down in 2009 to be rebuilt. The red carriage barn with attached ice house is on the south side of Broad Street. The ice house is now gone and the carriage barn has been converted to a residence at 59 Broad Street.

pushing and prodding they finally got it to the pasture, letting them continue on their way.

At about 7:00 P.M., with the summer sky still lit, the Lulls finally arrived at their new home at 60 Broad Street. They were exhausted. They pulled the mattresses off the wagon, laid them on the kitchen floor and collapsed to sleep for the night.

Hollis Home

Sixty Broad Street had three things that Marion had never seen before—a light bulb, a faucet with running water in the kitchen and a customized privy bench with two different sized seat holes instead of the usual one. The light bulb hanging from the middle of the kitchen ceiling won the grand prize of new gadgetry. They were each in awe over the simplicity of flipping a switch on the wall to fill the room with light. It was unbelievable—no kerosene, no match and no black soot.

The other jaw-dropping gadget was the water faucet above the kitchen sink. Marion could not believe that she didn't have to go outside to an open well, as she did many times in New Boston, to crank up the water bucket. Getting water in New Boston required jumping over a few more hurdles than it did in Hollis. In New Boston the open well behind their house was marked by a circular stone wall about two feet in diameter with a cover over the top to prevent anything, or worse anyone, from falling in. A foot above the well cover there were two foot long, horizontal wooden beams holding a rope with a hook on the end to hang the water pail. The well was about twenty feet deep and had probably been hand dug by the previous owner.

Getting water in Hollis was a whole different system. Here there was a windmill on the south side of the farm that pumped water from a deep well through vertical piping to more piping where it traveled a foot or so beneath the ground all the way from the windmill, under Broad Street, up to the cistern in the scaffolding of their barn. The cistern was a large open wooden tub to store well water. It had an incoming pipe to bring water

Arthur climbing down the windmill

from the well with two outgoing pipes; one which traveled down the barn wall, into the barn to provide water for the animals and another which brought water to the kitchen sink faucet. This fairly intricate system resulted in something so wonderfully easy—a simple turn of the faucet to get water that came from deep in the earth. A novelty the Lulls had never before experienced.

The third major attraction was the privy bench. This privy, unlike any other Marion had seen, was more than one size fits all. It actually had two seats—one for kid-sized bottoms and one for adult-sized bottoms; for Marion and Hilda, a most welcome idea.

Winter made the privy all the more entertaining. Freezing temperatures resulted in frozen waste, which meant Arthur could not shovel it out to the pasture far behind their house to bury it as he did in warmer months. Over the course of a particularly long winter the privy sometimes filled up so much that the waste peeked out above the seat surface, making for a challenging privy visit. On occasions such as this Marion looked more than forward to the first spring thaw.

Not that I want to stay on this subject, but I would like to pass on a noteworthy tidbit of information. In Marion's days of privies, toilet paper was something of the future. Toilet paper would not become an everyday item for another twenty years. So, until that time, they continued to make use of torn out pages from outdated Sears Roebuck catalogs or shelled corn cobs.

Three cheers for two ply and a flushing toilet!

Moving In

The day after the Lulls arrived in Hollis they were busy unloading the wagons, going back to Amherst for their stodgy cow and returning the horses and wagon to Mr. Hurd. A few days later, once they were somewhat settled in their new home, Arthur hired a man with a truck, Mr. Forace Lund, to drive him and Louis to New Boston to gather the few things they had left behind. Arriving in New Boston they loaded the truck with some heavy pieces of lumber along with a few other things. To their surprise, they also got something they knew would put a smile on Hilda's face— Puppy.

Just as the Lulls felt a hint of being settled in, Arthur received word that his jury duty was being changed from Nashua to Manchester. This was not good news. To get to Manchester meant traveling to Nashua by horse and buggy, paying to put the horse in a stable all day to then get on a train to Manchester. Unbelievably, Arthur once again faced the challenge of being able to get to the courthouse on time. He would have to leave by dawn each morning or perhaps earlier and he probably would not get home until well after dark. As arduous as jury duty was proving to be, Arthur, like the other jurors, had no choice but to make it work. The Lulls were not going to move again.

CHAPTER 4

School Life, Home Life

Starting School, Again

Marion never went to school in New Boston, but now that she was eight years old she knew she would have to go. Excited about going, when she saw the school for the first time, the idea of baking bread with her mother didn't seem like such a bad thing. The first time Marion and Hilda saw the school in Hollis, which was the Farley Building on Main Street, it left a lasting impression on each of them. After attending a one room schoolhouse in New Boston, the Hollis school stuck them as being large and imposing. Hollis's school had roughly 120 students while the one-room schoolhouse they were accustomed to had a whopping 12.

The Farley Building was Hollis's one centralized school known throughout town as the High School. The High School was built in 1877, which in large part was made possible with funds donated by a longtime Hollis resident, Mary Farley. Hollis was in great need of a new high school as its fourteen district schools, or one room schoolhouses, scattered around town became increasingly difficult to manage with overcrowding. Years later, the High School's name changed to the Farley Building when Hilda made a motion at town meeting to rename it the Farley Building in honor of Mary Farley's generosity. The motion passed.

The Farley Building

Marion expected she would be ready for school this time. Figuring her flour barrel days were long gone, she gathered her bravery to take on the challenge. While she hoped the butterfly in her stomach was from excitement rather than fear, she could not help feel apprehensive about being in a school with ten times more students than had been in New Boston. That aside, she was eager to meet new friends.

The High School housed grades one through six on the first floor and seven through twelve on the second floor. Marion liked the fact that the older kids were upstairs. It made for a less intimidating school day. Starting school in the 3rd grade classroom with six 3rd graders and six 4th graders, Marion liked her teacher, Miss Lucinda Read, who had a solid reputation of being a good teacher in addition to being very nice. Miss Read taught in town for many years, starting at the white, clapboard, one room schoolhouse on Ranger Road called the Pine Hill School or #3. (It still stands on Ranger Road and is owned by Marion's daughter.)

A few months into the school year, with Marion doing just fine, Miss Read had an accident that caused her to be out of school for three weeks. She had been riding her horse at home when the horse, trying to avoid a hole in the ground, jammed Miss Read's leg up against a split rail fence. The school tried unsuccessfully to find an interim teacher, resulting in the School Board's decision to divide her class between two other classrooms. The 4th graders went into a 5th grade room and the 3rd graders joined the 2nd grade in Miss Newton's room.

Miss Newton earned a rather different reputation than that of Miss Read. Miss Newton didn't smile much, if at all, which gave the kids all the ammunition they needed to refer to her amongst themselves as Miss "Biddy" Newton. Miss "Biddy" had an air of stuffiness that few could penetrate. To make matters worse, Marion did not learn a thing in her class. Although Marion didn't learn much from Miss Biddy, she made up for it in Miss Read's class. While doing her own work at her desk, Marion had one ear open to Miss Read's lesson to the older kids, essentially getting an educational two-for-one deal, learning two grades in one year. So, what might have appeared as a less than ideal situation actually turned out to Marion's benefit.

At lunchtime Marion and Hilda, along with the other kids who lived close to school, ran home for lunch. The students who lived too far away had to bring their lunch to eat at school. Considering the inequity of this, the School Board hired Mrs. Ora Brown, who lived down the road from the school, to make a large kettle of soup everyday for the kids who could not run home. They loved Mrs. Brown's soup. It made them feel better about not being able to go home for a warm meal.

I brought my lunch to school in a metal lunchbox. We didn't have a cafeteria so we ate lunch in our classrooms. My brothers and I still talk about the lunches we brought from home. When my mother started working full-time there was little time in the morning to pack lunches. Every Sunday evening we got out a few loaves of bread, a jar of Skippy's peanut butter and a jar of Welch's grape jelly to make a week's supply of sandwiches. We made sandwich after sandwich putting each one in a plastic baggy until the loaves were gone. Lastly, we stacked them in the freezer taking out a few each morning to bring to school.

Our PB&J sandwiches weren't your typical PB&J sandwiches—by the time we ate them the jelly side of the sandwich was blue. If you've never had a defrosted PB&J sandwich then you haven't had the sheer luxury of eating blue bread. I am amazed I still enjoy PB&J sandwiches, but then again they are not what they used to be.

The school day went from 9:00 A.M. to 4:00 P.M. with an hour break for lunch at noon. In the morning the children had a fifteen minute recess with another one in the afternoon. In winter, when darkness came sooner, school let out at 3:30 to give the kids time to get home before dark.

The dress code consisted of dresses or skirts for girls and knickers for boys. Marion, like the other girls, wore a skirt or dress with stockings, lace up ankle boots and a bow in her hair. Girls wore dresses most all the time as few owned a pair of pants. The boys wore a collar shirt, knickers, long knee socks and tie shoes.

One particular boy, named Doug Verder, whose nickname was Quacky Boy, made a lasting impression on Marion when he surprised her from behind, putting his hands around her neck in what he probably intended to be playful. Well, Marion thought it anything but playful. She never forgot it. Telling her mother about it, Hattie said that Quacky Boy was probably trying to get her attention because he liked her. It was his way of flirting. If only he had known that, for Marion, his way of flirting broke the bridge it hoped to build. Marion would stay clear of Quacky.

Coincidentally, in their fourth grade class photograph, Quacky sits in the first row, second from the right, seemingly scheming his next attack as Marion sits innocently behind him.

> I had a Quacky Boy in 5th grade whose name was Gilligan. He put his hands around my neck during recess and I got in trouble for slugging him. Growing up with three older brothers I knew how to take care of myself. While I have, for the most part, always considered this one of my strengths, that day on the playground it landed me in a conference with the teacher.

Louis didn't go to school in Hollis after completing 8th grade in New Boston because he had fulfilled the requirement. He could have continued on to high school, but out of necessity, chose to work with his father full-time on their farm as many boys did at that age. During 8th grade Louis

4th Grade, 1919

Front Row, left to right: George Burton, Eugene Hills, Maurice Maxwell, Herbert Snow, Henry Hildreth, Leonard Bennett, Douglas Verder, Earl Wright

Second Row: Miss Lucinda Read, Bill Benjamin, Edith Reed, Catherine Hills, Grace Hills, Vera Flagg, Lillian Benjamin, Marion Lull, Viola Frost, Althea Nute

Back Row: Donald Hardy, Emerson Hill, George Ladd, Agnes Tacklin, Alice Bigelow, Dorothy Ladd, Agnes Goyette, (unknown) Lealey, Wendell Wilshire

missed several weeks of school due to troubles with his appendix, making it unclear if he would pass. In the end, he did. So, at age fifteen Louis began working seven days a week, all year long with his father to grow their farm. Taking on the identity of a farmer, Louis learned what it meant to make a living. His friends did the same, logging, blacksmithing, building, coopering or taking on other trades.

Arthur and Louis worked together increasing the farm's productivity better enabling them to make a steady living, providing far more security than would have been possible had Louis continued in school. Louis worked hard alongside his father. He wanted to prove to his father as well as to himself that he could do the work of a man. Arthur and Louis were a strong father-son team; they, like other fathers and sons, shared a bond as nurturing as it was necessary.

Boys who did not work with their fathers went to high school. Clarence Howe, Marion's classmate and future husband, asked his father in eighth grade if he could drop out of school when he finished the year. His father replied, "Yes, Clarence you can stop going to school, but if you do, you will have to work on the farm like a man." That sounded like a deal to Clarence so after eighth grade he quit school to start working on his family's farm.

He worked "like a man" for one year until the boy in him decided not to miss anymore swimming at Flint Pond or ice cream at Locke's. He dropped out of the farm to pick up school. He had had enough of missing the fun he saw his friends and siblings having while he worked with no time to play.

Hattie's Home-Cooked Meals

Hattie cooked on a large, cast iron cook stove she filled with wood every morning. It had a long, narrow compartment on the right side of the oven to burn wood, heating the cook top and oven box throughout the day. The oven had two shelves rather than the standard one, giving her enough space to bake bread and roast meat and vegetables at the same time.

Breakfast was Marion's favorite meal. It often consisted of leftover apple pie from the night before or leftover baked potatoes that Hattie would fry up with some of the solidified fat from the kettle she kept on the stove. Another favorite was plain bread and butter, which might sound blasé, but Hattie's warm homemade bread and butter were well worth getting out of bed for.

It took Hattie a few days to make butter. First, she filled a wide pan with sweet, rich milk from their brown and white Guernsey cow, placing the pan in the ice box for a day or two until a cream layer, sometimes a few inches thick, formed on the surface. Skimming the cream off the top with her wooden skimmer shaped like a half moon, Hattie transferred the thickened cream to the butter churn for Marion and Hilda to take turns churning. Putting their muscle to good use the cream slowly turned to butter. Throughout the process, Hattie periodically poured off the thin liquid buttermilk that pooled at the bottom of the churn. After an hour or two of steady churning, with all the liquid extracted, Hattie put the butter in a bowl to work it with a wooden paddle for a half hour or so, adding water as she went, until it was nice and smooth. She then added just enough salt for the perfect flavor.

Hattie made fried potatoes, sizzling them in a pan with slivers of meat from the frozen pig carcass hanging in the shed. It was usually Marion's job to cut the meat; a job she had no problem doing as it was just another part of farming life. Each spring Arthur raised a young pig to slaughter in December to add needed fat and protein to their diets through the winter months. After slaughtering the pig he would cut it from snout to tail to hang in the cold shed one half at a time, using the meat as they needed.

My only experience with pig meat is that which comes from a pretty package where the hint of actual pig is rather remote. This is one large difference between farming life and supermarket life. Marion grew up eating food directly from its source be it animal, fruit or vegetable whereas I, for the most part, only know food that has been handled by numerous people or machines. Most of the food I eat has as much marketing content as it does nutrient content. I recall Hilda commenting how beautiful supermarkets are with all their colorful displays and packaging. I think for her, the supermarket is a remarkable exhibit of food.

Hattie often made biscuits for breakfast too. Mixing flour, butter, milk and a pinch of salt she made dough that she then cut into circles with a biscuit cutter, placing them on a baking sheet to cook in a hot oven until they fluffed up into pockets of flaky biscuit. Marion loved eating them right out of the oven smothered in butter and jam.

Sometimes for a Saturday morning treat Hattie let Marion make doughnuts. She made the dough by mixing an egg with some milk to which she added three handfuls of flour from the wooden barrel, a spoonful of fat from the kettle and a dash of cinnamon. Patting the dough on a floured counter, Marion formed doughnut sized round pies, cutting a hole from each center. The doughnuts were a special indulgence, yet it was actually the doughnut holes that Marion liked best as she, Louis and Hilda got to eat these warm from the kettle. The doughnuts on the other hand they saved for Sunday morning.

Baked Beans

August through November was an especially busy time for the Lulls. They harvested the fruits and vegetables, cooked and canned the tomatoes, made jams, stored the carrots and beets in buckets filled with sand to keep through the winter, piled the apples and potatoes in barrels to put in the cool corner room of the cellar and prepared the fields for winter.

One of Marion's jobs was to help harvest the winter shell beans. She picked the beans through the month of September when the pods were striped, brownish-red and dry on the vine. After hours of picking the pods she put them on baking trays to sit in a sunny window until they became brittle. Once brittle, she spilled the pods onto the barn floor to gently crack them open with the back of a shovel, releasing the prized dark red beans. Hattie used some of the beans for cooking through the winter, keeping aside a few handfuls stored in sacks to keep dry until the next spring's planting.

Hattie's homemade baked beans came from a one-of-a-kind heirloom seed from her mother's family that had been handed down for generations. Heirloom seeds were a big deal; they were a familial agricultural stamp that passed from one generation to the next. Sometimes heirloom seeds were lost, as was the case with Hattie's shell bean seeds that never made it to Marion's generation. Not knowing how the seeds got lost, they presume the stored beans must have become moldy or been eaten by mice. Beans not planted within a year of being picked would not germinate so, if you overlooked saved beans, they would be useless, adding to the ever expanding list of extinct heirloom seeds.

My mother was not a cook in the sense that she made a lot of homemade meals or baked goods. She took full advantage of packaged foods that required little more than putting in a preheated oven. Nevertheless, some of my mother's cooking succeeded in being memorable. My brothers and I remember all too well one of our weekly staples. We fondly refer to it as Mom's Hotdog and Potato Special. Here is the much coveted recipe—

Mom's Hotdog and Potato Special
Servings – 5
Preparation Time – 3 minutes, maximum
5 hotdogs
5 hotdog buns
5 slices yellow American cheese
Mashed Potatoes (preferably instant)

Put the uncooked hotdogs in buns. Cover each hotdog with mashed potatoes topped with a slice of cheese. Place under the broiler. Remove, ideally, before the cheese turns black.

My brothers and I still get a good laugh talking about those famous cold-burnt-bun-and-cheese-dogs. I should probably cook them up someday for dinner, but then again why spoil a good thing.

Another family favorite was broiled grapefruit with honey. They actually weren't too bad. They beat the hotdogs by a mile. Like most things my mother made, they were as quick as they were easy. Just cut the grapefruit in half, spread the top with honey and broil. (Broiling was clearly my mother's preferred mode of cooking.)

Then of course there were the periodic trips to the Wonder Bread factory store. Now that was good living. We had a big old clunky freezer in the basement we stocked full of Hostess Cupcakes, Pink Snowballs, White Snowballs, Cherry Pies, Apple Pies and a bunch of Twinkies to wash it all down. As a kid, I did not at all mind the goodies in our freezer although now, I cringe at the thought.

Saturday Bath

Every Saturday after supper Hattie rolled the heavy round wooden tub, resting upright against the shed wall, into the kitchen to fill halfway with warm water from kettles on the stove. Saturday was bath night for each of the Lulls. Marion stood in the tub washing herself with a bar of soap and a cloth until Hattie washed her hair, trying not to tangle it. After Hattie rinsed Marion's hair, Marion dried herself with a towel, put on her bed clothes and went up to bed with her heated freestone.

After Louis and Hilda each bathed they also got their freestones before going upstairs to bed. Hattie and Arthur then took their turns in the tub. They sacrificed the comfort of their baths for their children, bathing last in what by then would be cool, dirty water. Standing in the tub with goose bumps in soapy, used water certainly did not lend itself to a soothing or clean bath. Heating clean water between each bath would have been far too time consuming. After Hattie and Arthur finished with their baths they dumped the water into the kitchen sink to then roll the tub back into the shed until the following Saturday when they would do it all over again.

Chimney Fires

By mid to late winter, chimney fires were a common occurrence. Soot built up on the inside walls of the stove pipe creating fertile ground for fire. The Lulls, like most families, became quite adept at fighting them. They knew as soon as smoke started pouring out from the stove that Arthur needed to get the ladder quickly to climb up to the roof to pour water down the chimney. Fortunately, they beat every fire, though they rarely beat the mess it made on the parlor floor.

The house I grew up in did not have a wood stove so chimney fires were never a problem however, our broiler was. My mother broiled steaks, which oftentimes caught fire from the fat being too close to the heating element. But no fear, my mother was always there roasting-pan-ready to suffocate the flames with the pan, inverting it over the steak. It worked like a charm every time.

A Tree in the Pasture

One Christmas, Marion wanted her family to have a Christmas tree so she set out to the edge of their pasture with an ax in hand. Walking to the far end of the pasture, to find what she hoped would be the perfect Christmas tree, she came upon a little cedar tree about four feet high with lovely green, wispy branches. She chopped it down, carrying it home to put up in the parlor. When Arthur saw the tree he said something like, "Oh, Marion, it's a lovely tree . . . a lovely Christmas tree, though it looks an awful lot like the cedar I've been saving to grow tall." Marion sunk into her shoes. She wanted to hide. Rather than surprising her family with a special tree, she stood there wishing she could rewind the minutes. Later that afternoon, Arthur walked out to the pasture to see which tree Marion had cut only to return with a big smile extending out from under his bushy mustache. He told her that she hadn't cut down his tree after all.

Looking back on this, years later, Marion thought she probably had cut down her father's tree, but being the

thoughtful man he was he did not want to diminish the
pleasure of her thoughtfulness.

> My mother patched something for me, as Arthur did for Mar-
> ion, when I was about ten years old. My grandfather (my
> mother's father) owned a cabin in the woods in Schaumburg,
> Illinois where we visited him a few times.
>
> Suffice it to say, my grandfather was a man of novel
> ideas. Whenever we visited him he loved handing out his
> prized collection of BB guns for us to shoot coffee cans off
> various tree stumps along the edge of the woods. I don't
> remember if I ever shot a can, I only know that the BB gun
> was about as big as I was. Nevertheless, we must have done
> a great job shooting because my grandfather actually had the
> gumption to send us home with our very own BB gun. I don't
> know what he was thinking and I certainly don't know what
> my mother thought or how we even got it home, I only know
> we had a big old scary BB gun tucked between her filing cab-
> inet and the wall in her small office at home.
>
> Years later, I came downstairs one morning to see a
> squirrel on top of our birdfeeder. I went to get the BB gun,
> like my brothers often had, to scare it away. The day before
> my brothers had run out of BBs so rather than go outside to
> scare the squirrel I just stood in the kitchen, lifted the gun,
> took aim and fired.
>
> Well, I don't know who I scared more, me or the squir-
> rel. I shot a BB right through the first pane of the sliding glass
> door leaving a little hole smack dab in the middle. I guess it
> wasn't out of BBs.
>
> I went upstairs to tell my mother. She got out of bed with-
> out saying a word as we went downstairs. Looking at the hole

in the glass, she wrinkled her mouth to one side and said, "I've got just the thing." She went to the pantry to get a roll of red and white checkered sticky contact paper, cutting out a daisy-like flower that she then stuck onto the glass over the hole. Voila. That was that. Problem solved.

Gifts in the Hall

By Thanksgiving every year the Lulls received a delivery of Christmas packages from Hattie's cousin, Zola, who lived in Goffstown. Zola was clearly ahead of schedule when it came to Christmas. Marion had the hardest time seeing the brown paper wrapped packages sitting by the front door day after day from Thanksgiving all the way to Christmas. It took all the discipline she had to refrain from opening them. Each day her anticipation grew. The days and weeks seem to drip on forever.

Finally, on Christmas morning they were allowed to open their gifts. Zola always sent the children two gifts, each wrapped in pretty paper with a shiny bow. One gift was always practical while the other was for fun. Marion remembered one Christmas she got a book and a pretty white dress, Hilda got a pencil set and a xylophone and Louis got a brand new Swiss army knife. The knife counted as two gifts. Cousin Zola's gifts absolutely made Christmas. Well worth the long wait, Marion treasured her gifts and treated them as such.

Hilda's Pony

Hilda loved animals. When she was fourteen years old Arthur decided to swap one of his cows to get her a pony. Although the cow provided milk and a bit of income, Arthur wanted to surprise her. He arranged the trade with a man in

Pepperell, Massachusetts, who walked the several miles to Hollis with his pony in tow. When the pony arrived, Arthur harnessed it in their barn without Hilda's knowing and then called to her in the house to come take a look in the barn. As soon as she saw the black pony she knew what her father had done. She would never forget it.

Crabby

The Lulls' hens were all fine, as were the eggs, but they had one rooster Marion appropriately named Crabby because it was not fine. Whenever she went out to the barn to collect eggs, bad Crabby would come running at her ankles as if they were chicken feed. On one particular crisp morning, Marion went outside to get eggs for breakfast, walking proudly in her new green velvet dress that Hattie had recently sewn for her, when sure enough Crabby came at her flapping his wings. As Marion lifted her foot quickly to shoo him away she fell flat on her bottom in a mud puddle. Running inside in disgust, Hattie appeased her emotions saying they would clean up her dress like new.

Slop Jars and Chamber Pots

Marion had a few jobs every weekend as did Hilda and Louis. Other than making their beds every morning Marion was responsible for pouring the dirty water from each wash bowl, in each of the three bedrooms, into the slop jar. The slop jar was nothing more than an empty jar to contain the dirty water. Next, she cleaned the chamber pot in each bedroom, emptying its contents into the privy, rinsing each one out with the slop jar water.

Hattie's Everyday

The first summer the Lulls lived in Hollis, Arthur worked at Brookdale Fruit Farm for Charles Hardy, the grandfather of Eleanor and Elwin Hardy. He planted apple tree seedlings, on land now occupied by Brookdale Farm Stand, earning about two dollars for an eight hour day. They were long days, but the money he earned put food on the table.

Hattie worked hard cooking, cleaning, laundering clothes, sewing and keeping a garden. In managing the children and the house she established an efficient routine to ensure everything got done. Monday was laundry day. She first washed the colored clothes in a large tub of cold water, scrubbing each piece with a bar of soap before rinsing them in another tub filled with clean water. After hanging the cleaned clothes on the line outside, she then washed the white clothes and bed linens in a tub of boiling water, stirring them with a long wooden stick.

In the wintertime it would be a stretch to say the clothes and linens hanging on the line actually dried; froze would be more accurate. But, like most things, Hattie was a woman of solutions. Before taking the rigid clothes and linens off the clothesline to bring into the house, she gave them a good whacking with the back of a shovel to soften them up before spreading them out in the parlor to thaw.

I think I'll go kiss my Kenmore.

Tuesday was ironing day. She got out the heavy flat irons, warming them repeatedly on the cook stove, to press the clothes and linens crisp. Just as Arthur relied on Louis to take on day-to-day responsibilities, Hattie relied on Hilda and

Marion to do the same. When Hilda was about fourteen years old it became her job to iron the handkerchiefs. With time, she took on more ironing responsibility as did Marion when she came of age.

Wednesday was sewing day. It was a day for darning holes in socks, patching knickers, repairing torn seams and sewing dresses for the girls. Hattie typically made the girls' dresses from hand-me-downs she received from her cousin that she carefully took apart at the seams to cut and sew into new dresses using her treadle sewing machine. As nothing was ever wasted Hattie used all the fabric, making the dresses for the girls and then, with the leftover scraps piecing together little matching dresses for Hilda and Marion's rag dolls.

Thursday was cleaning day. Hattie shook the rugs outside, washed the front windows and scrubbed the floors on her hands and knees with a rag. Living close to the road posed a constant fight against the ever invading dust that invariably made its way into the front of the house. Road dust was so pervasive it warranted three town road agents, one of whom was farmer Lewis Rideout, to periodically pour oil on the Hollis roads in an attempt to keep the dust under control.

On Fridays and Saturdays Hattie, with Hilda's and Marion's help, cooked and baked. Making as much as she could in advance to ease each day's meal preparation, Hattie made, at a minimum, two fruit pies, three loaves of bread and a large pot of baked beans to have throughout the week.

Sundays were for church, visiting with friends and enjoying a large meal at noon. Everything in town was closed, though you could buy a Sunday paper at Norman Bennett's house at Four Corners (now the site of the Country Kitchen).

Other than church, a meal, the paper and daily farming chores, Sunday was a day of relative rest.

Church Hymns

Hattie had a soothing habit of singing church hymns as she went about her house work. Hymns became part of who she was at a young age from hearing her own mother sing hymns. And, even though Hattie's mother died when she was just five years old, singing hymns lived inside Hattie just as they had for her mother.

Hannah Follansbee

After Hattie's mother died she went to live with her father's parents, Benjamin and Hannah Follansbee, because her father, working full-time, couldn't take care of her. Hattie grew up under the care of her Grandma Follansbee who, although a serious, somewhat petulant woman, was also a giving soul. Mothering Hattie as best she could, Grandma Follansbee taught her how to play the pump organ and sing hymns, giving her the gift of love, care and music that would stay with her for the rest of her life.

Music had a special place in my family too, most significantly, Mitch Miller's Christmas album and singing hymns at church. I have fond memories of standing next to my mother in church while she belted out songs better than she ever gave herself credit for. Singing Christmas hymns together was our all-time favorite.

My mother died of Alzheimer's in 2002 and when my husband, children and I go to the Christmas Eve service at our church in Nashua, I miss her most. Singing "Hark, the Herald Angels Sing," I can see and hear my mother belting it out with a smile on her face as if she were standing next to me. It's one of those bittersweet moments when I embrace her presence while, at the same time, I endure her absence.

CHAPTER 5

Louis

Hanging On

At sixteen years old, Louis endured twenty-five days at Memorial Hospital in Nashua due to serious problems with his appendix. Bent over in unbearable pain, Arthur brought him to the hospital as quickly as he could. After an agonizing, fearful ride to the hospital the doctor told them that Louis had appendicitis. He needed surgery to remove his appendix as soon as possible. With little time to waste, Dr. Smith and Dr. Wallace would operate on Louis the following morning. Arthur and Hattie feared for his life.

Leaving home early the next morning, they drove the horse and wagon to the parking stable near the bridge on Main Street, then walked many blocks in the snow to be with Louis at the hospital. While the doctors operated, Arthur and Hattie waited anxiously through each and every dripping minute hoping he would survive.

Much to their relief, Louis came through the surgery, though his recovery was still tenuous. The doctors and nurses kept a watchful eye on him around-the-clock, not allowing any visitors, including his parents. Arthur and Hattie wanted nothing more than to see their son, but having no choice, they walked back down Main Street to get the horse and wagon to ride home. At day's end Arthur opened his diary to write, "January 21, 1920—This is a sad day for us."

Over the course of Louis's hospital stay Arthur went to visit him nine times with Hattie joining him most days. One day they asked their neighbor, Effie Flanders, whose son was a good friend of Louis's, to join them. Another day when Arthur couldn't go, Hattie drove the team of horses herself. After Louis had been in the hospital for about a week Arthur finally brought Marion and Hilda to see their brother. On February 3rd Arthur wrote in his diary, "Louis is getting stronger in his voice and could sit up a short time." Then, on February 15th Louis was well enough to go home.

Had Louis not survived the ordeal with his appendix, the future of the Lulls' family farm would have been at great risk. Arthur could not do it alone. At fifty-five years old and counting, he did not have the capacity to give the farm the vitality it needed to carry on. For this reason, Louis's recovery served as a turning point in the life of the farm as it would be his strength and determination that would fuel the farm's longevity.

CHAPTER 6

Making a Living

Ice Business

The day before Louis went into the hospital with appendicitus, Arthus purchased an ice business, from a local man by the name of George Ladd, to help make ends meet through the winter. Although he and Louis had no experience cutting or selling ice, they would learn. If others could do it, so could they.

As soon as Silver Lake froze about a foot down Arthur and Louis went out on the ice with their horse Molly to get to work. They rigged Molly with a plow to clear the snow off the ice and then, replacing the plow with a platform of sharp points, they scored the ice into large blocks for cutting. Following the marked lines, they sawed a couple of inches into each block to make the initial cuts.

With the initial cuts made, they could then stab an ice pick around the edges of the block to split it deeper. They then shimmied a sharp, short pole under the block of ice to leverage it just enough to get it onto the end of a ladder. Next, they used an ice ax to push the block of ice up along the ladder to the wagon. With the wagon full of ice, the team of horses pulled the heavy load to the ice house at the Lulls' farm where it was unloaded and stored between generous layers of sawdust.

Molly getting ready to score the ice—1922

The ice business was a hazardous job that required unrelenting strength and focus. Just standing on the ice posed danger enough, never mind being on it with a horse and heavy equipment. Fortunately, Arthur and Louis were lucky. The only mishap they ever experienced was the day Molly fell through the ice close to the shore where the men were able to pull her out.

The Ice House at Lull's farm attached to the carriage barn

For the first two years of the business Arthur managed delivering ice to their customers until in his late fifties the weight of the ice became more than he could handle. Louis took over, bringing ice to people all over town beginning with deliveries in January, working into September

Loading the truck

when surprisingly, the ice blocks remained frozen hidden in sawdust in the ice house. On Tuesdays and Saturdays Louis parked the wagon in the center of town chiseling off chunks of ice from blocks to sell to people who needed it to put in their metal ice boxes. On the days he didn't sell ice in town he sold it at their farm.

By the third year of the business, Arthur and Louis's hard work paid off. They had enough money to afford themselves the luxury of a truck to transport the ice. In addition, Louis, in his usual ingenuity constructed his own fuel-powered ice saw to cut through the ice. With these conveniences, Arthur and Louis had the tools they needed to grow the business.

The summer camps along Silver Lake and the Locke family, who operated an ice cream business out of their house at 5 Broad Street, were Arthur and Louis's primary customers. The Lockes bought the most ice. One August Louis delivered 17,660 pounds of ice to Leslie Locke at twenty-five cents

The wagon ready to deliver ice

per 100 pounds, for a total of $44.15 (about $561 in today's dollars). Locke's homemade ice cream was the best you could find for miles. Made from fresh cream and berries, the ice cream drew people from all around Hollis as well as surrounding towns from early spring into the fall. And the price was as good as the ice cream. At ten cents for a generous dish, or about $1.25 today,[2] it didn't take long for the Locke's business to outgrow their house. They built an ice cream shop off the south side of the house, expanding their operation to meet local demand.

> My favorite ice cream growing up was Brigham's chocolate chip with jimmies. Every so often my friend Martha and I walked or rode our bikes a mile and half to get a medium Brigham's cone for twenty-five cents. The Brigham's Ice Cream shop was across the street from the movie theatre where we went to see movies for seventy-five cents a ticket.

Cutting ice at Silver Lake

Louis Lull, on left, and Horace Morrill at Silver Lake. Ice saw fabricated by Louis Lull.

A dollar worked out perfectly. The other downtown attraction was Barbra Jeans. It was actually the main attraction. It was a candy store that did a booming business just with the kids on our street. My brother used to buy 100 mint juleps for fifty-cents. You can't beat half-penny candy. I liked the price of mint juleps, but I didn't like how they stuck to my teeth. I

Locke's Ice Cream, 1921

opted for colored candy dots on a white strip of paper, twiz-
zlers and fireballs. They had ice cream too, but we never got
it there because the lady of the store scooped it. We were afraid
of her.

An Acre a Day

The ice business contributed significantly to the Lulls' financial stability in that it provided an economic cushion, on top
of the farm, that made them far less vulnerable to the risks of
operating a single venture. In the winter, income from fruit
and vegetable farming was limited to the sale of winter
squashes, canned vegetables, jams, apple cider and if haying
was done—piles of hay (neatly packaged bales of hay didn't
come until years later). The Lulls sold very little if any farm
products through the winter since the ice business generated
the income they needed to make a solid living.

In early spring Arthur and Louis started the farm work.
The first priority was plowing the fields to prepare them for
planting. Louis did most of the plowing with the team of

horses pulling the plow back and forth churning up the dry winter beaten grass into long raised rows of brown, fertile soil marking the beginning of another growing season. Louis usually plowed an acre a day, which was a good day's work considering it was done with a 15" plow blade, two horses and one man. (Interestingly, the word "acre"[3] was first defined by the area that a yoke of oxen could plow in a day.)

Cutting Hay

Arthur and Louis spent many summer days cutting and pitching hay in the fields. It was a vital part of the farm because it fed the animals. It was also used for bedding in the stalls and pens. They cut the hay pulling a wide sickle-bar mower through the tall, cornbread colored grass one width at a time. With the field mowed Arthur and Louis then used hand scythes around the periphery to cut hay the mower missed.

Louis plowing an acre a day

They left the cut hay on the ground to dry in the sun for a few days before raking it into piles to be pitched onto the wagon. While it lay on the fields drying Arthur and Louis used teddars and pitchforks to fluff it up, helping it to dry. Otherwise, the hay could get moldy, making it unusable. Once the blanket of hay was dry they raked it into piles, polka-dotting the entire field with little haystacks.

Apples and Peaches

Each year Arthur and Louis planted more apple trees as well as peach trees to expand the small orchard they started with. Arthur's work at Brookdale taught him the business of apples that he knew, from experience, had promising profit potential. But growing fruit was not easy. To be successful required an understanding of the science of plants and pollination. Fortunately, Arthur and Louis had that knowledge. They also had the land they needed to make orchards a

Arthur on wagon, Marion center and Hilda on the right

Arthur and Louis spraying trees

prominent part of their farm, in the hope of realizing comparable profit.

They planted, they fertilized, they sprayed, they pruned and they hoped. They hoped for sufficient rain through the summer to nourish the maturing trees. They hoped for warm, sunny autumn days to bring growth and cool nights to bring rest, giving the fruit optimal growing conditions. The weather greatly affected the health of an orchard. Where optimal growing conditions made a bumper crop, poor conditions resulted in a bum crop.

Barn Cellar

In the wintertime the cows remained stationary in the barn standing side by side in stanchions with a bar on each side of their neck to keep them in line. Their manure collected in a wide gutter embedded in the barn floor behind them. As the gutter filled it automatically flipped over, dropping the manure to the cellar below. The barn cellar served two purposes. It kept the manure away from the cows, keeping the barn relatively clean and it provided space to store the manure until farmers needed it to fertilize their fields in early spring.

Through the winter the manure piled up, which in most cases was not a problem, but at times it resulted in colossal damage. Where a little moisture did no harm a lot of moisture could be catastrophic. The accumulating manure in the barn released a fair amount of humidity, compromising the strength of the barn floor, especially an old one.

Marion knew of a couple farms in Hollis where rising moisture from the barn cellar softened the barn's wooden floor planks to the point of collapse. Soft wood and heavy cows were not a good combination. When a floor gave out the confined cows inadvertently hung themselves.

Spring Milk

As soon as the grass in the pasture grew a few inches high, Arthur let their seven cows out of the barn to roam free for the first time in months. After being cooped up in their stanchions through the winter without interruption, the cows came out of the barn with stiff, unsteady legs. For most, the first order of business was to rub up against a tree or a split rail fence to scratch themselves, in many cases, to the point of bleeding. Being outside for the first time allowed the cows the pure bliss of attending to a winter's worth of itching. Marion never liked seeing the cows bleed though she came to understand it as a sort of spring rite of passage.

The process for letting the cows out to graze was a gradual one. The first day Arthur let them out for just an hour or so to give them time to slowly regain their field legs as well as adjust to eating grass. Each day they grazed progressively more over the course of roughly a week and a half until they were left to roam all day.

In the spring, as the cows' diet changed from hay to grass, their milk took on a distinctly different flavor. Essentially, the milk had two annual flavors—Winter Hay and Spring Grass—each with its own taste Marion clearly remembers taking a few days to get used to.

Clean milk cans out to dry

CHAPTER 7

Seasons

Waterfalls and Flowers

Each season brought different things for kids to do. In spring-
time they looked forward to walking across the fields from
Lull's farm to Van Dyke Road to see the water flowing at Van
Dyke Falls. Marion and her best friend, Althea Nute, along
with their other good friend, Viola Frost, often went there
to take pictures of each other in front of the small waterfall
created by the brook water running over the top of a boulder.

Another teenage favorite thing to do was to go "mayflow-
ering" in the woods off Wheeler Road. The kids could almost
close their eyes following the sweet-smelling scent in the air
to come upon a shady glade where large patches of small,
white fragrant mayflowers grew in abundance. The kids loved
to come pick the flowers, breathing in the fresh new per-
fumed smell of spring. It was a tradition many looked forward
to. The kids also shared the annual event by surprising
housebound folks around town with bouquets of mayflowers
so they too could enjoy the pleasure of spring.

Summer Picking

Marion worked in the summer along with lots of other kids
picking strawberries for Mr. Harold Hardy. They started picking in June as soon as the strawberries were ripe, frequently

getting dismissed early from school to pick the berries before they went bad. When the kids got out of school for the summer they picked the berries from five in the morning until noon, filling one box after another. It didn't take long before the kids amused themselves by making a race out of it. Two kids started at the beginning of a row, one across from the other, picking like wild fire to reach the end of the row first. The only rule was that you had to pick all the berries without skipping any.

Throughout the morning, Mr. Hardy walked the rows telling the kids, "Don't skip any berries," as he collected their boxes, keeping a tally of how many they each filled. They earned three cents per box with a bonus of being allowed to eat a few handfuls of berries while they picked.

The kids picked strawberries through the month of June until the rows were picked clean. Then they moved on to the next ripe crop. After strawberries came the peas and then the string beans. The beans were the hardest to pick because you had to practically rip the whole plant out of the ground to get a bean off the stalk. One bushel took forever to pick bringing only a few cents reward. In August, picking was all about peaches, blackberries and corn. After that came the apples, squash, potatoes, beets and carrots.

Another source of income for Marion came from the big old chestnut tree behind their house where she collected the scattered chestnuts to sell by the roadside. Setting up 'shop' in front of the house displaying her baskets of shiny chestnuts she sold all she could to people passing by. One particularly profitable year, Marion earned enough money to buy herself a brand new pair of shoes for $1.95.

Strawberry and Box Lunch Socials

Every summer the Strawberry Social that was held in the center of town drew a progressively larger crowd. A core group of local women, who managed the majority of the preparation as well at the event itself, got up to their necks in strawberries for several weeks. Two weeks before the Social the women rallied as many people as they could to volunteer picking strawberries at Brookdale Fruit Farm. Groups of people picked and picked until they filled Mr. Hardy's large flatbed wagon with baskets of succulent, red ripe strawberries.

With the wagon full, Mr. Hardy brought the load of strawberries to the Congregational Church where the women rinsed, hulled and sliced them. Rinsing went rather quickly compared to the tedious job of hulling and cutting. Pulling the green calyx crown from the top of each strawberry needed some good town gossip to keep momentum. After hulling, the naked berries then went to the cutters who sliced them one by one, pint by pint, bushel by bushel, filling what must have been just about every bowl in town. The last step was dusting the berries with sugar, letting them sit until the day of the Social. The women also made hundreds of shortcake biscuits. Strawberry shortcakes were a big seller. People looked forward to them year after year. (The Strawberry Social is one event from Hollis's past that still stands strong today, thanks to that local group of women who began what has become the Women's Club. Today's "Strawberry Festival" is much the same as years ago although now the berries come from both Lull Farm and Brookdale.)

The Box Lunch Social was a popular event for teenagers. Girls made special box lunches at home to bring to the

Strawberry Social, 1918

center of town where boys bid on their favorite lunch. The highest bidder of each lunch won the privilege of sharing it with the girl who prepared it. For some this served as an opportune time to start a crush, keep a crush or, in some cases, end a crush. Either way, it was an annual event enjoyed by the teens.

Peaches

Marion must have had a competitive streak because one time she bet a friend that she could eat more peaches than he could. Although Marion managed to do quite well in the bet she also managed to give herself quite a plump-ugly-peach stomach ache. She succeeded in eating eighteen peaches, accumulating an impressive pile of pits while her friend lagged far behind. It was a bet Marion never forgot. It also put an immediate end to her betting days.

The Loft

Many afternoons Marion, Althea and Viola played in Marion's barn attached to the house. They had an exciting time climbing up the ladder to the loft to jump down into a big pile of hay. One time Marion fell into the hay just missing four newly born kittens. They couldn't have been more than a few days old. She carefully put them in her dress pocket with a handful of hay to bring them into the house to show Hilda, the Lulls' self-made veterinarian.

Hilda brought the kittens back to the barn where she made them and their mother a nest of hay tucked away in a safe area of the barn. The kittens somehow knew instinctively to stay in their nest until they grew big enough to roam outside. When they were old enough to drink from a saucer, Hilda gave them milk each morning and afternoon until they were able to fend for themselves, catching mice or other little vittles to eat.

Another favorite thing the girls did was put on plays in the loft in the carriage barn. They would make up scripts, rehearse for several days and then invite their mothers to see their show. The girls put their hearts into it, which made the shows well worth going to. Marion's mother always came to watch as did Viola's, but unfortunately Althea never enjoyed the opportunity to perform for her mother. When Althea was just five years old her mother died. Knowing very little of her mother, Althea's relationship with her was defined more by the missing than the memories. And in that missing she connected to her.

Silver Lake

Marion loved to go swimming at Silver Lake with Althea and Viola. At the beginning of one summer Marion didn't have a bathing suit, which you would think might be a problem, but for Marion it didn't amount to more than a bump in the road. Lack of a bathing suit was not going to put a crimp in her style. She ingeniously figured that if her rag doll had a bathing suit made from leftover fabric then why couldn't she? Marion asked her mother if they could make a bathing suit from the wool skirt that was now too small for her. Hattie thought it was a fine idea.

> It's a good thing Hattie and Marion didn't try to make a bathing suit from the skirts walking around these days. That would have been quite a sight.

Wild Winter

In wintertime, the kids loved skating and sledding. As Hilda recalled, "winter vacation was a great time to go skating on the pond in our cow pasture on Wheeler Road. The two Lovejoy girls helped us learn to ice skate and we sure did enjoy this. We also went sliding on the crest of a hill on our field. After a big snowstorm when men had to shovel out big drifts on Lovejoy Hill, and the snow was somewhat tramped down, I remember sliding with a few of our neighbors down the middle of the road all the way to Dow Farm where there is a big old red barn opposite Van Dyke Road. Once, when the roadway was icy, I seem to remember that we even went as far as the large old farm beyond the second hill."

I asked Hilda's daughter, Sue, to clarify the distance for me as I wanted to clock it in my car. She told me it was from the top of Lovejoy Hill, where there's a large yellow house with attached barn at the corner of Pine Hill Road and Broad Street (formerly the Lovejoy house) to the bottom of the second hill at 162 Broad Street. That's a long way. In fact, it's 7/10ths of a mile. Wow. That's good sledding.

Back then, there were no trees on the hill so this record-setting distance was possible. They enjoyed a great ride, but because it took so long to walk back up the long hill they only had enough time to squeeze in a couple of runs before it got dark.

Snow drifts on Broad Street

I remember well the winter my most adventurous brother made an igloo. Waking up to a snow day with high drifts on each side of our street, left by the plows, he saw an opportunity not to be wasted. Using a shovel he built a dome about four feet high and six feet across from the tall drift of snow. With the dome complete he then made a small doorway to shovel the snow from the inside to hollow it out. He then got our garden hose from the basement, attached it to the exterior faucet of the house and turned it on to gently soak the igloo leaving it to freeze overnight.

The next day we woke up to a solid snow-ice dome. It was fabulous. To finish it off he found a rug scrap in the basement to lie on the igloo floor, making it a most comfortable home away from home. It was a neighborhood sensation.

Ice skating on Hildreths' pond (Marion is third from the left)

CHAPTER 8

A Car and a Bus

Louis's Car

Louis was diligent about saving what earnings he could which, with time and patience, afforded him the practical indulgence of buying himself a used, but plenty new enough, Ford Model T touring car, commonly called a "Tin Lizzy." Although Lizzy cost him a whopping $512, wiping out his hard earned savings, he could not imagine putting his money anywhere else. He liked machines. Lizzy fit the bill. Plus, he would be one of the few people in town who owned a car.

Dr. Hazard, who was the only doctor in town, was the first person in Hollis to own a car. He lived in the house on

Louis's Ford Model T in front of their house

the corner across from the Town Hall. When Marion was about thirteen years old she developed a fever that warranted a house call from Dr. Hazard. He arrived at the front of their house in his car, leaving a lasting impression on Marion. Relatively unconcerned about her fever, he told her to stay in bed and to drink lots of cambric tea. The medicinal tea consisted of hot water mixed with a spoonful of sugar and a dash of milk. In no more than a few days Marion's fever passed.

> *My doctor's name growing up was Dr. Powell. He lived in a gray two story house with his office on one side. We went there each year to get our annual physical exams. He had one secretary and one exam room. I liked Dr. Powell. He was a nice man. My guess is Dr. Hazard was too. But with a name like that I'm glad I went to Dr. Powell.*

Radio Days

Soon after Louis bought Lizzy he drove all the way to Boston to buy something else not many people had—a radio. He came in the house with what looked like a small wooden cabinet about the size of a bread box and turned it on. The Lulls were nothing short of amazed to hear people having a conversation. How odd to hear voices other than their own fill the room. It was a strange but wonderful phenomenon. Their new radio provided entertainment they had never experienced. The first night they had the radio Arthur and Louis sat up until two in the morning listening to a radio show. Hattie didn't take to the radio like the men in the family did. She preferred singing her hymns.

I also had something growing up that was a novelty. When my parents bought our house in Newton, Massachusetts, it came with something that you rarely see. Although for us it was part of the house like anything else, I suspect others might have been a bit surprised to see the head of a moose, antlers and all, mounted on the wall in the front hallway.

My brothers used to tell me the rest of the moose was behind the wall. I think I believed them because I liked the idea that, although it wasn't alive, it was whole.

Our moose could have been just a moose, but in our house he was "Andrew." Andrew was a pet of sorts. My mother used to like dressing him up for the major holidays. On Valentine's Day, she'd put a big, floppy pink hat wedged between his two big furry ears. On July 4th, he wore a white Styrofoam hat with a red, white and blue ribbon and on Christmas, he went formal with a black velvet hat and a red bow tie. He also had an unlit cigarette in his mouth until my mother made him quit when smoking became unfashionable.

School Bus

Louis Lull had drive, literally. He frequently thought of ways to earn money. When he was twenty years old it occurred to him that he could probably make a job for himself by transporting kids to and from school. He went to the Selectmen to ask if they would pay him to do this. They agreed. Monday through Friday, Louis hitched the horse up to the sleigh or wagon, depending on the weather, to bring the kids who lived along the two mile stretch of Wheeler Road to school. He picked up about eight children each day. The kids loved

Another Hollis "school bus" similar to the one owned by Louis. One of the students posed for the photograph. (This "school bus" was owned by Maud Hale.)

being driven to school although on bitter cold days the ride felt uncomfortably long.

Louis's driving job turned out to be a steady business that led to bigger and better things. After the first year of driving the horse and wagon he prudently invested in purchasing Hollis's first official motorized school bus. Both he and the town benefitted. Parents liked the idea of their children being driven to school, especially in bad weather. The community welcomed Louis's school bus.

Thinking ahead Louis rightly believed that if he could be busy driving one school bus then he could probably profit from another so, he bought another bus, hiring a friend to drive a second route.

I never rode a bus to school. From kindergarten through 12th grade I walked to school as did all the kids in my neighborhood. The only school bus I experienced was the one that brought kids from Boston's inner city to our school. I think the first year it came I was in the fourth grade; it was 1969. My friend Mimi lived in Boston. She came on that bus, but unfortunately we never had the opportunity to play after school because she had to go home on the bus. I don't recall Mimi after 6th grade. I believe they stopped bringing kids from Boston that year.

Louis with a student in front of Hollis's first motorized school bus

CHAPTER 9

High School

Best Friends

Marion and Althea met in third grade, wasting no time becoming best friends. They did everything together—skating, sledding, swimming and acting in plays. In high school they went to basketball games, the movies and dances. Their lifelong friendship carried them through school, work, marriage, children and everything in between.

In grade school Marion learned a little about what life might have been like had she not had a mother at home. On Saturday mornings when Marion was often in charge of getting the cows from the barn to the pasture on Wheeler Road, Althea frequently joined her. Once in the pasture, Althea would go ahead of Marion, crossing the street to the East Cemetery where her mother was buried. Going to her mother's gravestone she would lie down in front of it, crying into the grass. Over time, as the grave settled it left a depression in the ground where Althea's intimate ritual

Althea and Marion

clearly spoke of the space in her soul. Marion just let it be. She never said a word and neither did Althea. It was just one of those things that they both knew was there, but where silence worked better than words.

Althea's gravestone ritual brings up an experience for me that is actually a nice memory. In grade school my mother period-ically brought me and my brothers to the Woodlawn Cemetery in Wellesley, Massachusetts, where we would have a picnic lunch at my father's gravestone. It was always peaceful there. I liked that we were, in a way, visiting my father. My broth-ers and I played tag, weaving around the headstones. When I was tall enough to reach the gas pedal in the car my mom let me drive for the first time. I think I was about twelve years old. My brothers and I each learned how to drive at the ceme-tery. It was actually a good place to learn—the worst we could do was hit a headstone.

Thinking about this now, I realize how difficult visiting the cemetery must have been for my mother, a single mother with four young children who went to the cemetery to sit at the headstone of a man they all loved. But being the woman she was, she rose above her sadness, and ours, to create some-thing truly special for all of us. From our cemetery picnics, stories of my father and letting us know how lucky we were to have the father we did, she brought lasting joy where you would least expect it.

Soon after Althea's mother died, her father, Mr. Nute, who had a job working long days at Brookdale Fruit Farm, needed to find someone to take care of his daughter. He asked a good friend of his wife, Ferma Locke Lovejoy, about the possibility of taking Althea in. Ferma's compassion coupled with her husband's ability to support their six children, by means of his profitable blacksmith business, provided all they needed to welcome Althea into their home. She moved in sharing a room with Hazel who was three years older than her to slowly become part of a new family.

A couple years later, Althea's father met a woman named Miss Stephens who worked at a hair salon in Nashua. They ended up getting married at which point Mr. Nute moved to Nashua while Althea stayed with the Lovejoys. Althea rarely saw her father, but she did visit her stepmother a few times each summer when she, Marion and Viola were allowed to go to Nashua to see a movie.

Marion, eighth grade

Going to the movies was far from simply getting in the car to drive a few miles. For them it involved running, and a lot of it. First they ran eight miles to the Nute's house at the south end of Main Street (near Hayward's Ice Cream) to get their hair washed by Mrs. Nute and then they ran to Granby's Movie Theatre back up Main Street. After the movie they ran all the way back home to Hollis.

I wonder how Marion, Althea and Viola would do in the Hollis Half-Marathon. I can't imagine running sixteen miles in my best running shoes and apparel, never mind in soft shoes or lace up boots. Growing up we rode our bikes everywhere and everywhere was never more than five or six miles away. Marion didn't own a bicycle because at that time they were a luxury most could not afford. So Marion, like the other kids, ran all over town, going to school or basketball games or, in some cases, the movies.

Dances

Marion started going to dances as a freshman in high school when Louis offered to drive her to one of the two dance halls at Silver Lake. Wallace's Grove was at the south end of the lake. Morrill's Grove was at the north end. Every Wednesday and Saturday night there was a dance going on at one of the halls and many times at both. Young soldiers, sixteen to eighteen years old who were in training at Camp Devens in Ayer, Massachusetts, came to the dances in a camp bus. The bus load of young men, dressed in their starched uniforms and black shiny shoes were probably a welcome sight to Marion and her friends. In those days dances were all the rage.

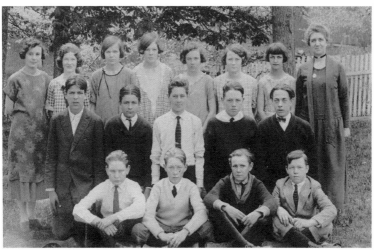

High School Freshman Class, Hollis, NH
Front row left to right: Henry Hildreth, Edmund Dickerman, Bill Benjamin, Benedict Hogan

Second Row: Donald Hardy, Edward Szlosek, George Ladd, Clarence Howe, Wendall Manning

Back Row: Teacher-Miss Westhaven, Marion Lull, Helen Sullivan, Dorothy Ladd, Elizabeth Pineo, Althea Nute, Viola Frost, Teacher-Miss Welton

Young men and women, all dressed in their finest, dancing to live music created an energy like no other.

The boys had to buy tickets at the door using one ticket each time they asked a girl to dance. Each dance really counted. The first boy to ask Marion to dance was George Ladd whom she knew well from school. After the dance the kids liked to walk over to Wallace's food stand to treat themselves to a steaming hot dog in a warm soft roll, smothered in soft boiled onions. It was a fine ending to a fine evening.

Dancing and going to local plays were an integral part of most communities. The Lulls, especially Marion, gained a

solid reputation in each. Throughout high school Marion performed in town plays, oftentimes with Ralph Bascom who was
equally talented in getting audiences to come back for more.

In Hilda's words, "We loved going to plays put on by the
Grange or the Women's Relief Corps. The Odd Fellows
always sponsored a Thanksgiving Dance and a New Year's
Dance. The Grange was a nice thing to join as it gave the
young people something to go to every month. The Grange
was a farming community organization that sponsored very
popular costume balls as well as other social activities for
folks of all ages at the Lower Town Hall. After each of the
Grange meetings they usually danced to the piano played by
Mrs. George Ladd. The Grange also sponsored a fair in the
fall showing garden vegetables, food tables, livestock and
poultry. The exhibits, mostly done by 4–H groups in town,
were displayed in the Town Hall."

Basketball Games

At age 16, Marion earned thirteen dollars one summer picking for Harold Hardy. That's a lot of boxes and beans. As a
reward, she set out on her first shopping spree. The first thing
she bought was a book of basketball tickets to go to all the
high school games at the Upper Town Hall. The high school
basketball games drew a large crowd. Students, parents,
teachers and townspeople filled the auditorium to cheer on
the teams. It was clearly the place to be, especially on a Friday night.

Back then, the high school didn't have a telephone so if
a game had to be cancelled due to the weather, one of the
players would run to Davis & Goodwin's Red and White

Store across the street from the high school to call the other team. If the other team needed to cancel, they would call the store and the clerk would run up to the high school to let them know.

After buying the basketball tickets Marion ran all the way to her favorite store on Main Street in Nashua, Woolworth's, to buy a Christmas gift for each person in her family. She bought tissue paper for Hilda, a roll of string and a red bandana for her father, a spool of thread for her mother and for her brother she splurged on a shaving mirror that cost twenty-nine cents.

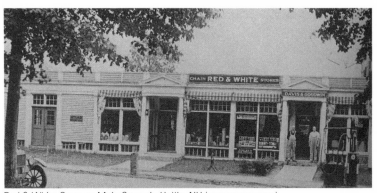
Red & White Store on Main Street in Hollis, NH (now apartments)

Graduation

Marion graduated from high school in June 1928, in a class of eleven students. She was valedictorian. Clarence Howe was salutatorian. Marion and Clarence never competed for first place so his being salutatorian was not a problem until you added his mother, Lottie Emma, into the mix. When Lottie found out that Clarence was salutatorian and not valedictorian, she called the high school thinking they must have made a mistake. They graciously recounted the grade points with the same result. Clarence never raised an eyebrow over his graduating rank. He had plenty to be proud of, with perhaps one exception—his mother's call to the high school.

For graduation Marion wore a white silk dress with a satin ribbon sash tied around her hips with a large bow on one side. Her accoutrements included a long pearl necklace, white stockings and white shoes. The ceremony began at the high school with the students walking in formation to the Town Hall where they received their diploma rolled up in a pink satin ribbon.

Marion's graduation picture

The girls carried small bouquets of peonies grown and arranged by Mary Wilson who cultivated the flowers every year in her garden specifically for graduation. (Mary Wilson lived in the red house just south of today's Hollis-Brookline high school sign. As it stands now, it is hidden behind climbing vines and large shrubs.)

$2 a Day

After Marion graduated from high school she got a babysitting job working for Mrs. Stella Hardy earning $2 a day. She would arrive in the morning to take care of her young daughter, Eleanor, a precocious two year old who consistently tried to follow her older brothers and sisters to school. Eleanor did not like being left behind. Marion quickly learned that unless she wanted to wrestle Eleanor she had better figure out a way to distract her. Thinking on her toes, Marion managed to get Eleanor interested in the horse in the barn while the others went off to school.

While keeping an eye on Eleanor, Marion started each day preparing a hearty dinner, served at noontime, for the five Hardy children and the hired farm workers. Marion peeled, mashed, kneaded, rolled, roasted and baked—cooking various meats, vegetables and breads. Mrs. Hardy took Marion under her wing, teaching her excellent housekeeping skills.

Marion worked intently at the Hardy's for a year until she took a job at the Lincoln Store in Nashua as an office clerk earning ten cents an hour. It would be less money, but it would also be less work. As a clerk, Marion counted the register money, typed purchase orders and mailed invoices.

The Lincoln Store gave Marion a sense of camaraderie that she did not get working at the Hardy's. Being the socialite Marion was, she preferred her job at the Lincoln Store, though looking back years later she knew it was the Hardy job that served her well in the years to come.

CHAPTER 10

Arthur

Pa

It was a sunny, but very cold day Hilda remembers well.

"Pa asked me to drive him to Flint Pond where Louis was cutting ice. He wanted to see how Louis was doing. They went across the street to the carriage barn to where the car was. It did not start so Pa had to turn the crank a few times before it started. This was not good for his chest. When they arrived at the pond, Pa got out to help Louis. About twenty minutes later he said, 'Hilda, you must be cold. You go home and I'll get home with Louis in his truck.' I said, 'all right.' I did not think to say that I was not cold and could stay longer. That was a big mistake.

It was about an hour and a half before Louis started for home. When Pa came in the house his face was very red. Ma gave him a hot drink of tea. He sat beside the kitchen stove for about one hour. After a while he decided to lie down on the couch where he usually slept in the front room. We were all rather late getting to bed. Marion had to work late at the store.

The next morning Ma got up about 7:00 to start the fire. As she passed Pa on the couch she gave a cry. He had died sometime during the night. I remember she hollered to us upstairs—'Children get up your father is dead.' It was a shock to all of us. We called our neighbor, Arthur Davis, who called the funeral parlor. Ma did not want his body taken away so the undertaker did their work at the house. Mrs. Davis invited Ma and us to come over to their house to stay. We decided to have the funeral after a couple of days. Many neighbors came."

Before Marion left to go to the Davises she walked over to Arthur to gently lift his spectacles off his face. Then she walked upstairs to her bedroom and placed her father's glasses in a small drawer in her dresser. She wanted to keep some of her Pa. As she put the spectacles in the drawer she said to herself that she would never speak his name again. That way, she would hold him inside forever.

Daguerreotype of Arthur Lull as a boy, 1865–1930

Marion held onto her father's glasses like I hold on to a beautiful green leather scrapbook my mother made for me and my brothers to remember our father. It opens with a letter from my mother that she wrote to us soon after my father died. I treasure that letter because it connects me to my father through my mother. The book is a collection of letters people sent after my father died, various pictures of him, Navy papers and a short secret code he made up.

Like Marion, I also hold my father inside though I do speak his name. My husband and I named our daughter after him.

For several days after the funeral, Hattie sat in the rocking chair in the front room where Arthur died. She did not cook or clean or do much of anything. She rocked. Marion and Hilda made a few loaves of bread. Louis, on the other hand had enough energy for all of them. He held onto his father by working harder than ever, in an unfailing determination to keep their farm alive. He planted sweet corn for the first time and he added all the apple trees he could afford to expand the orchard. Louis not only wanted to preserve the farm, carrying on what his father started, he also wanted to strengthen it.

As part of Louis's plan to firmly establish their farm he decided it was due time to give the farm something it never had—a name. No longer would it be merely known as the Lulls' farm. From now on their farm would be—The Red Fruit Farm. In hanging up a sign, Louis's naming of the farm made a bold statement to the community. What might have appeared as a seemingly small gesture, in essence was Louis's decision to commit the rest of his life, just as Arthur had done, to what was now, The Red Fruit Farm.

CHAPTER 11

Money and Love

Grandmother Lull's Money

Now that Marion was twenty-one, the money that Grandmother Lull had put in the bank for her when she was born was hers. Louis and Hilda enjoyed the satisfaction of getting their money, but Marion on the other hand, did not. Marion turned twenty-one in 1931 amid the Great Depression. Money was not to be had. Banks were failing one after the other causing many people to lose most or all of their uninsured savings. Marion was one of them.

If things had gone as planned Marion would have received $100 plus interest. She received $37. Far less than what she had hoped for, it still provided the means for Marion to do for her mother what Hattie could not do for herself. Marion went shopping. Her mother would soon be the proud owner of a state-of-the-art electric washing machine and refrigerator.

May I Have this Dance?

Marion and Clarence Howe started school together in eighth grade when he decided that going to school was better than "working like a man" on the farm. Clarence grew up on his family's farm on what is now Howe Lane. The Howes had a few dairy cows, a crop of corn, field feed, several laying hens, a small variety of fruits and vegetables and several work horses. Their farm, like many family farms, operated several ventures simultaneously. This way, if one failed it didn't bring the rest of the farm with it.

Through middle school and high school Marion and Clarence were classmate friends until, ironically, after leaving school, things between them began to change. While Marion worked as a clerk at the Lincoln Store, Clarence worked with his father on their farm. Other than their work, they often saw each other at dances around town. Clarence knew Marion liked to dance, but more importantly he knew he wanted to dance with her. So, he asked her on their first date.

Their dating life began when they were twenty-two, and, for the most part, it involved dancing. They went to every dance offered, traveling to Manchester, Nashua, Bedford and Milford, kicking up their heels wherever they could. Marion always looked forward to each dance. In her words, "I always wore a pretty dress and Clarence always ironed himself a clean white shirt. I liked how sharp he looked."

It did not take long for Clarence or Marion to realize that they were not only impressive dance partners, but perhaps life partners as well. When Clarence asked Marion to marry him she did not skip a beat in saying yes. There was only one hurdle Clarence wanted them to clear before the big day. Being the practical man he was, he wanted them each to save $800. He believed it would be irresponsible of them to get married without saving first. He somehow figured that after they each saved $800 they would have what they needed to start a life together. Marion didn't question the task, she simply committed herself to it.

Hurricane

A fierce hurricane swept through New England on September 21, 1938. The unnamed storm, as hurricanes weren't named until 1950, killed 685 people (six from New Hampshire) and caused about five billion dollars of property damage in today's dollars. In New Hampshire, the worst of it came between 5:00 and 6:00 P.M. when the strongest winds measured ninety miles per hour in places with torrential downpours of up to ten inches. Electric power and telephone service were out for up to two weeks, mail delivery was suspended for days, hundreds of roads were blocked and thousands of bridges and dams were destroyed. In Weare, four women died when a bridge collapsed over the Piscataquog River. In Peterborough, the Contoocook River flooded resulting in a fire that wiped out the entire business district.[4]

In Hollis, the hurricane's fierce winds brought trees down all over town creating an ugly "game" of pick-up-sticks that lasted for weeks. The large elm tree in front of the Lulls' house fell over incurring costly damage to their roof. Power lines, telephone lines and even utility poles came down everywhere making roads impassable. Marion was stuck at work in Nashua unable to drive home, with no way of telephoning Hattie to let her know she was safe. Luckily, she happened to see her neighbor walking home who told her that he would stop in at Marion's house to let Hattie know she was alright.

Most of the apples in the Lulls' orchard were scattered all over the ground. To salvage whatever they could the entire family spent several days picking up the apples. One morning out in the fields, they saw the most monstrous bon-

60 Broad Street

Trees and phone lines down in front of the carriage barn and in front of their house at 60 Broad Street

fire they had ever seen. Mr. Hardy had gathered all the fallen debris from his property to burn in one immense pile about fifteen feet high. The flames and crackling were impressive.

The hurricane left everyone scrambling to get their lives back in order. Houses and barns were in need of repair, fallen trees needed to be cut and power and utility lines needed to be reinstalled. In the resulting chaos of the hurricane, the Lulls were most concerned about the damage caused by their fallen elm. The total cost of needed repairs would be about $600. It was money they did not have. One of their ice customers did owe them close to what they needed to fix their house, but they could not bring themselves to ask for it when everyone was trying to get back on their feet. So the Lulls, rather than acting on what they needed, acted out of silent consideration. They would not repair their house. They would sell it.

They sold it along with a five acre parcel on Wheeler Road that included a small apple orchard and Lull Pond, to Alan and Beryl Orde for $3,000. The Lulls kept the cow pasture on Wheeler Road as well as the rest of the farm on the south side of Broad Street. With the sale of 60 Broad Street, Hattie was able to pay off the balance of what they owed Ms. Farmer as well as renovate the carriage barn for her, Louis, Hilda and Marion to move into.

The deed for their remaining property had each of their names on it, but because Hattie had never before owned anything of significance independently, she asked her children if they would sign a portion of the deed over to her. For once in her life she wanted to have something to call her own. Louis, Hilda and Marion gladly signed the carriage barn over to their mother.

Louis's Tractor

Louis loved machinery. He often got his hands on seemingly worthless equipment that he had a knack for bringing back to life. Seeing a beat up, broken down tractor at another farm

Carriage House, 59 Broad Street, after being converted to living quarters

in Hollis, he asked the owner about it who told him the tractor would never work, but he would sell it to him to use the parts. Louis didn't skip a beat. He bought the tractor at a bargain price of $35.

After working on that monster of a tractor for weeks on end, to the amazement of many, perhaps himself included, he succeeded in getting it going. Once again, Louis proved himself a prudent investor. His refurbished gasoline powered tractor was proudly the first used for farming in Hollis.

With the tractor, the work Louis previously completed in a day now took half the time. Hauling cow and pig manure along with fertilizing, cultivating and plowing the fields proved much more efficient. The days of the horse drawn plow working the usual standard of an acre a day were over. But it would not be like Louis to leave the tractor at that. He wanted more. In his entrepreneurial manner, Louis knew he could plow a lot more than only Red Fruit Farm. He began plowing fields all over town generating the income he had envisioned from the start.

Growing Red Fruit Farm

After Arthur died, Louis managed to keep the ice business going for another eight years. Then, as electric refrigerators and freezers becoming increasingly commonplace, the business of selling ice soon melted. Louis knew when the Locke's invested in a sizeable freezer chest his ice business had suddenly become obsolete, making winter income a problem. Rather than take on something new, Louis put his bets on something he already had—Red Fruit Farm. Figuring he had the land, equipment, drive and determination he needed to make a living off the farm alone, Louis put his heart and soul into what he knew best.

Louis and his tractor

He planted rows and rows of apple trees. He planted peach trees. He planted more corn and he planted more vegetables and fruit trees. Expanding the orchards yielded fruit Louis sold from house-to-house and Hattie sold from low bed trailers at the farm. Soon enough their fruit sales brought in what their ice no longer could.

Louis's decision to put all his efforts into the farm served as a critical turning point in the farm's future. Had he not developed the orchards and vegetable crops as he did, Red Fruit Farm, in all likelihood, would not have had the substance it needed to survive. Louis knew what he was doing and he did it well.

Hattie selling peaches at the carriage house

CHAPTER 12

Marriage and War

Eight Hundred Dollars

After working eight years at the Lincoln Store, Marion finally saved $800 to contribute to her and Clarence's prenuptial savings. They could finally get married. And so they did, on September 30, 1940.

> *Coincidentally, I also married on September 30th, though I did not save $800 beforehand. I admire Marion and Clarence for their discipline. For them, life was clearly about saving money more than it was about saving time. Money did not come easily. They used and reused everything possible. Waste did not exist; neither did 'spending money.' There were no extras. There were no extra clothes strewn on the bedroom floor or spare shoes or coats in the closet. There were no extra goods or gadgets. They had what they needed and all they needed they had.*

A year before Clarence and Marion married a foreclosed house went up for sale on Ranger Road. Knowing such houses could sell at an attractive price, Clarence did not hesitate making an offer on the house. He saw the sale as a once-in-a-lifetime opportunity that he could not forgo. Although the bank's listed price was $2,000, or twice as much as

Clarence and Marion on their wedding day

Clarence had, he figured he had nothing to lose. He offered $1,000, which the bank accepted.

Marion and Clarence didn't move into their house right away as it was in serious disrepair. Measuring 26' by 28' with three small rooms, this small house sat on forty sprawling acres of land. Twenty-six acres on the house side of Ranger Road with the remaining fourteen acres on the other side of the road.

The previous owners had taken down all the interior doors, chopping them up for kindling wood and they left a big hole in the ceiling. The house also had no bathroom. They could use the privy at the end of the shed, but they chose not to because being so close to the house, the odor, particularly in the summer, would be foul. Marion relieved herself at the far, open end of the barn cellar where she often saw Puff Adder snakes that puffed up near her. These checkerboard patterned snakes lived around the granite foundation of the shed and barn making visits to the "privy" consistently unpleasant.

Home on Ranger Road, about 1950

Chicken Farm

Clarence made a living in the poultry business he shared with his brother, Norman, raising more chickens than you can imagine. While some fields around town were known by their cows and others by their orchards, Marion and Clarence's were recognized by their chickens. Clarence and Norman divided their labor. Clarence took care of the chickens. Norman took care of the eggs. Clarence built the chicken houses and incubators, raised the chickens and slaughtered them while Norman candled and packed the eggs for retail.

Norman candled the eggs in the basement of his house holding each one up to a bright light bulb to see if it had a blood spot. Any egg with a blood spot indicated possible fertilization and thus, could not be sold. (Candlers first used the light of a candle to detect fertilization or abnormality. In commercial processing, candling is done to grade the quality of the eggs. Candlers look through each egg to determine the thickness of the albumen or egg white as well as the shape of the yolk. Eggs that have a thicker albumen and a more oval yolk are of highest quality or Grade A. These eggs are for household or retail use while Grade B eggs are for bakery operations. Grade C eggs are used for nonfood egg products.[5])

Marion managed the bookkeeping for the business in addition to managing the house. She no longer worked at the Lincoln Store because, following company policy, once she married she had to leave her job to make it available to a single woman. Marion would have continued at the Lincoln Store had she been allowed to. She enjoyed the camaraderie working there that she knew would be difficult to replace on Ranger Road. Marion could have grumbled, but in her usual go-get-it attitude she rose to the occasion.

The first year Clarence and Marion were married they scraped by on earnings of about $400. They stretched every dollar as best they could. The needed house repairs and renovation absorbed their savings leaving them with almost nothing. Money was so tight they did not even buy a Nashua Telegraph for two cents a day.

As time went on, their chicken business slowly accrued some savings. Over the years, Marion and Clarence accumulated eight chicken houses that each spring held a total of

12-week-old chickens roaming
the range on Ranger Road

about 500 chicks. The chickens roamed within a fenced in area of the field that each year Clarence rotated to give them new pasture; leaving the used area fallow for two years to regenerate. Each night the chickens knew instinctively to scurry into their respective houses. Then, safe in their houses Clarence did his chicken rounds closing each door to keep the foxes and hawks away.

Hilda Marries

Hilda married Henry Hildreth in 1939. She moved out of the carriage house and into the Hildreth's family home at 16 Broad Street, continuing her work as an operator at the Hollis Telephone Company owned by Henry's father. Hilda says, "Henry was a bashful man," though he did have the sensible gumption to ask her to the movies one Thursday evening. Going out that Thursday, and the next, and many thereafter,

Henry soon asked Hilda to marry him. In Hilda's words, "Henry was a quiet, conscientious man. He never bragged and he didn't fool around with cards. He worked hard." They married, living happily ever after sharing their mutual modesty, love of the outdoors and quiet ways of accomplishment.

When Henry and Hilda married, Henry was working as a lineman for the electric company in Pepperell. When his father died in 1943, he took over the Hollis Telephone Company acting as manager, lineman, installer and night operator. Sometimes Hilda assisted Henry setting telephone poles by driving the truck while Henry leveraged each pole using cables attached to the truck to lift it into a deep hole.

Other than Henry's commitment to the phone company, he earned the distinction of becoming a fifty year volunteer member of the Hollis Fire Department. In this regard, Henry followed in his father's footsteps who had also been a fifty year member, seventeen of which he served as the Hollis Fire Chief.

Henry and Hilda shared a mutual enjoyment of the outdoors, especially walking in the woods. Even back then he, along with a handful of people, had the foresight to do whatever they could to preserve wooded land parcels for everyone to enjoy. Henry worked with Jeff Smith and Hollis Nichols researching property deeds to identify parcels that had been abandoned by owners who had moved away or who hadn't paid their taxes. These abandoned parcels became much of what is Beaver Brook today.

Hilda certainly enjoyed the woods, but her real love was animals. She and Henry had a large backyard where, over the years, Hilda became a shepherd of sorts with goats, bunnies, cats, plenty of kittens, dogs, ponies and chickens.

In 1944, when Hilda was thirty-six years old, she had her first and only child, Sue Ellen. They still live in the same two-family house at 16 Broad Street where Hilda once took care of Sue and now Sue takes care of Hilda who is a remarkable 102 years old.

Henry died on his seventy-sixth birthday in 1987 from complications of Parkinson's disease. His daughter recalls her father as a "kind, gentle man." She liked the idea that when people moved to town, Henry, coming to their house to hook up the telephone, was often the first person they met. "I think meeting him was a nice introduction to Hollis."

As Henry lay in the hospital days before he died, his family told him that the voters at Town Meeting had just approved the funds for a new fire station to be built off Ash Street. As a faithful volunteer fireman for the better part of his life, he could not have been more pleased.

Louis Marries

Louis married Grace Hague in 1943. He was forty, she was thirty-six. She moved out of the house where she grew up on Depot Road in Hollis to move into a rented house with Louis. Louis moved from the carriage house, leaving Hattie alone for the first time. The first few years Grace and Louis were married they rented several different houses until moving into the white clapboard house they had built at 65 Broad Street in 1947 (next to the current Lull Farm Stand).

Throughout their marriage Louis managed the farm while Grace taught school in Scituate, Massachusetts, and later Littleton, Massachusetts. They had no children. He and

Grace socialized with Grace's circle of friends, playing board games and other things Grace liked to do. Where Grace led, Louis followed. You could safely say Grace ruled the roost. She was a woman with clear ideas and intent without much room for indecision.

War

Just over fourteen months after Marion and Clarence married, the United States joined British forces in World War II. Fortunately, because Clarence and his brother Norman were established farmers, contributing to the provision of food as part of the war effort, they were not drafted. As much as it was a saving grace that they did not have to go to war, they did feel a sense of loss staying home while other men went off proudly to fight for the United States.

As there were those that fought, women too joined the charge, albeit less directly, doing what they could from home. Marion did the bookkeeping for the poultry business and Hilda volunteered as a spotter of warplanes at the watch tower on top of Warren Towne's Hill on Ridge Road. (Warren Towne was Hollis's fire chief at the time, leading generations of Towne's who have since followed.) Hilda worked the six-hour morning shift with Dot Hardy, Harold's daughter, watching for war planes from the top of the tower. If ever they spotted a plane, they immediately called the operator in Hollis from the telephone hooked up at the tower. The operator then called the government office in Boston, to alert the authorities there.

Becoming a volunteer spotter required completing a training class to learn proper identification of warplanes and flight patterns. In the watch tower, spotters indicated in a log book each type of plane, its flight direction and the time it was seen. In all the hours Hilda spent in her two years as a spotter she made only two calls to the operator.

Hilda Lull and Dorothy Hardy Twichell on duty

CHAPTER 13

Marion

"Are You Someone I Should Know?"

The transition Marion faced when she left the bustle of work to be a housewife on quiet Ranger Road took patience and perseverance. After moving from the carriage house to Ranger Road, she often took it upon herself to walk four miles each way to visit her mother or to see friends. Although she did not have a car, she did have two strong, need-to-see-some-people legs that gave her the ability to be with others. Whenever she was home at Ranger Road she always caught whoever might be walking by to chat with them. Her standard greeting of, "Are you someone I should know?" worked every time.

It occurred to Marion that she and Hilda might have been better suited to each other's lifestyle. Hilda, who was perfectly content with her animals, would have done well living on a farm as Marion did on Ranger Road and Marion, who liked to be social, would have enjoyed the town life where Hilda was on Broad Street.

Marion eased her early sense of isolation by keeping busy. She tended her large garden, kept an orderly house and managed the accounts for the poultry business. A meticulous bookkeeper, she kept a weekly tally of every expense, business and otherwise, even tracking Christmas purchases down to the last two cents for wrapping ribbon. Marion was also a resourceful housekeeper. She made curtains for all the windows from grain bags, stenciling blue flowers along the edges, in her effort to create a pleasant home.

Children

Marion and Clarence had their first child, Stephen Lull Howe, in 1943. Two years later they had their daughter, Sharon Mae Howe. Stephen and Sharon grew up at 60 Ranger Road where Stephen, who is handicapped, still lives today.

After Stephen was born Marion sensed that something had gone wrong. However, because she was under general anesthesia she had no way of knowing for sure. Her doctor gave her no information. While he might have very well had none to give, Marion did hear two stories of what possibly occurred. Nonetheless, with or without the stories, she would never learn the true cause or causes of Stephen's handicap.

Ferma Lovejoy, who had taken a course in nursing to help with deliveries at the hospital, told Marion that she had seen a nurse drop Stephen by accident soon after he was born. Someone else at the hospital told Marion that when she went into labor, a nurse called the obstetrician at home who told her to tie Marion's legs together to delay the birth until morning. Marion could not speak to either incident. She only knew that her son suffered brain damage that would affect him for the rest of his life.

In Marion's day, women and babies were traditionally kept in the hospital for ten to twelve days after the birth. On Stephen's tenth day at Nashua Memorial Hospital he had a

seizure that lasted for three days. He also developed pneu-
monia, precluding surgery to release the fluid around his
brain. Stephen had hydrocephalus, which required care
beyond the scope of that available in Nashua. Marion and
Clarence brought their son to Children's Floating Hospital in
Boston in the hope specialists there would be able to help.

Much to their disbelief, Marion and Clarence felt
Stephen's care in Boston inexcusable. He did not receive
nearly the attention they expected. With all they were going
through they were additionally faced with having to see
Stephen a mess in his crib from a badly soiled diaper that
went unchanged. The doctors informed Marion and
Clarence that, sadly, there was nothing they could do for
Stephen as he had little chance of making it.

Well, Stephen did make it. He made it due to the unfailing care of Marion and Clarence and later his younger sister,
Sharon. Although Stephen is crippled as a result of hydrocephalus and unable to care for himself, as a child he did
learn to walk and he did attend school. At school, when he
felt a seizure coming on he would ask the class to turn away
saying, "Don't look." He did not want them to see him in
the throws of a seizure. Stephen had seizures all through
school until finally, when he was eighteen years old, medi-
cines to minimize seizures became available.

Stephen and Sharon started school in the first grade;
Stephen at the high school, referred to as the Farley Build-
ing, and Sharon at the Town Hall because by that time the
Farley Building had become overcrowded. After first grade
Sharon's large class of about thirty students moved to a newly
completed six room elementary school on Silver Lake Road

where they stayed through sixth grade. After sixth grade they went to the Farley Building. In high school, Sharon's senior class would be the last to attend the Farley Building. One month before school ended, her class moved the entire contents of the Farley Building to the newly built high school, currently Hollis-Brookline Middle School, to graduate from there.

Stephen managed relatively well through elementary school because his mother's diligence in teaching him how to read gave him the ability to, for the most part, keep up with much of the work. In high school, however, things changed. The work simply exceeded his capabilities. Stephen did his best to learn what he could. Lacking special education services to assist him or cultivate his abilities, he did not achieve what might have been possible. As a senior in high school, although he had not been able to do much of the course work, because no one had told him otherwise, he fully expected to graduate with the rest of his class. A few days before graduation, the principal informed Stephen that he would not be able to graduate. He needed to stay in school an extra year. Stephen was crushed, as was Marion, Clarence and Sharon.

The following year Stephen did finish school but he left with a heavy, broken heart. After all he had been through the principal gave him a Certificate of Attendance rather than the diploma he had always hoped for.

Bake then Cook

Marion did everything she could for her children. Her attention to them as well as to the additional responsibility of cooking and cleaning more than filled each day. Meal preparation alone consumed a good portion of her time. The family ate their largest meal at noon, having a light supper in the evening. Their midday meal consisted always of meat and potatoes with a seasonal vegetable. Potatoes came with every main meal because they grew in abundance and stored well in the root cellar all year long. Marion usually prepared mashed potatoes unless short on time, boiled potatoes sufficed.

As with most families, Marion relied on her garden for a good portion of their food. When a vegetable became ready to pick, they saw it on their plate twice a day for at least a couple of weeks until that one was gone and the next one was ready to harvest. First they ate asparagus until it came out their ears, and then it was on to peas. Sharon didn't mind the peas so much because while helping her mother shell them she was allowed to eat some fresh from the pod. After peas came summer squash and beans, then tomatoes and cucumbers, then corn, then shell beans, then potatoes and last, winter squash. Blue hubbard squash was a particular treat not because it tasted better than the others, but rather because it had nubbly skin and it was so hard that Clarence needed an ax to split it open.

Breakfast usually consisted of oatmeal or an egg on toast. Eggs were an important staple. Not only did they provide much needed protein, but they were also an important component in Marion's love of baking. Where cooking meals was a necessity, baking was pure pleasure. Marion routinely made a variety of cookies, cakes and pralines that she happily shared. She often baked batches of her favorite raisin cookies filling a basket to bring to the summer parties they had down by their pond. Marion was, among other things, known for her baking. Every Christmas she made box upon box of assorted candy and pralines to give to friends and family. She took baking to the limit. At the age of ninety-five she made her specialty Christmas pralines for, unknowingly, the last time.

Soft Raisin Drop Cookies
"My mother's favorite and mine also."
Marion Lull Howe

Marion learned this recipe from her mother. She also submitted it for inclusion in the Women's Club cookbook of 1975.

Yields 4 Dozen

2 C raisins	4 C flour
1 C water	1 tsp baking powder
1 tsp soda	1 tsp cinnamon
1 tsp salt	½ tsp ground cloves
1 C butter	½ tsp nutmeg
2 C sugar	1 tsp vanilla
3 eggs, beaten	

Boil raisins and water about five minutes. Cool and add the soda and salt. Cream butter and sugar and add eggs. Sift dry ingredients. Mix all together, plus vanilla. Drop by large tablespoons on a greased cookie sheet. Let dough set a few minutes before baking. Bake at 350 degrees for about 15 minutes, depending on size.

Inexpensive Sponge Cake
Betty Crocker's Picture Cookbook

This cake, often called Mock Sponge, Butter Sponge or Hot Milk Sponge Cake, is quick and easy. Marion used to make it when she was working at the Lincoln Store. She always made it with Broiled Icing. It is one of Sharon's favorite cakes.

For Large Cake

- Grease and flour two 9" layer pans or one 13" × 9" oblong pan.
- Beat with rotary beater until very light. 4 eggs
- Beat in 2 cups sugar, ½ tsp salt, 2 tsp. vanilla
- Beat in 2 tbsp. butter melted in 1 cup boiling hot milk
- Sift together and beat in very quickly 2 cups sifted Softasilk or 2 cups sifted Gold Medal flour and 2 tsp. baking powder

For Small Cake

- Grease and flour one 9" square pan or 12 muffin cups (lined)
- Beat with rotary beater until very light. 2 eggs
- Beat in 1 cup sugar, ¼ tsp salt, 1 tsp. vanilla
- Beat in 1 tbsp. butter melted in ½ cup boiling hot milk
- Sift together and beat in very quickly 1 cup sifted Softasilk or 1 cup sifted Gold Medal flour and 1 tsp. baking powder

Immediately pour into prepared pan. (Fill muffin cups ⅔ full.) Bake cake at 350 degrees. Bake cupcakes at 400 degrees. Bake until cake tests done (about 25–35 minutes for cake and 18–20 minutes for cupcakes). Cool. Serve fresh with fruit and/or sweetened whipping cream.

Broiled Icing
Betty Crocker's Picture Cookbook

13" × 9" oblong pan	9" square pan
Mix together . . .	
6 tbsp. soft butter	¼ cup
¾ cup brown sugar	½ cup
4 tbsp. rich cream	3 tbsp.
½ cup nuts, cut-up	⅓ cup

Spread over top of warm cake. Place about 3" under broiler (low heat) until mixture bubbles and browns. For extra goodness, add about 1 cup Wheaties or moist shredded coconut. (Marion always made it without the Wheaties or coconut.)

Old Fashioned Pralines
Marion Lull Howe

In a heavy, medium sized saucepan over medium heat, add:
1 box light brown sugar
2 Tablespoons butter
⅓ cup whole milk or light cream

Heat, stirring constantly until thermometer reaches 240 degrees (you can also test if it's done by taking a small spoonful and dripping the mixture onto a saucer. The mixture should fall in a thread.) Then add 1 teaspoon vanilla and 1–2 cups whole pecans. Stir to combine and drop by spoonfuls onto waxed paper on countertop. Work quickly before candy hardens (if it hardens add a little more milk). Shift wax paper so it doesn't stick to countertop.

Doughnuts
Hattie Follansbee Lull

2 eggs	3½ cups flour
2 egg yolks	½ teaspoon nutmeg
1 cup sugar	1 teaspoon salt
¾ cup milk	6 teaspoons baking powder
¼ cup cream	1 teaspoon lemon extract

Sift flour, nutmeg, salt and baking powder three times. Beat whole eggs and yolks slightly, add sifted sugar, milk, cream and extract. Stir in dry ingredients. Chill dough or let set overnight before using. (I usually have to use a bit more flour). Roll dough out about ½" thick. Form into doughnuts. Fry about one minute on each side in deep fat (Crisco or Spry) 370 degrees.

Cream Puffs

On special days when Hattie had extra eggs she let Marion and Hilda make cream puffs.

½ cup flour	¼ cup butter
¼ cup water	¼ tsp. salt
¼ cup milk	2 eggs

Cook water, milk, butter and salt in a pan until it boils. Add the flour, stirring constantly. Stir until all the liquid is absorbed and the dough pulls away from the sides of the pan. Put dough into a bowl to cool for several minutes. Then add eggs, one at a time mixing well after each egg. When the dough is smooth, drop it by the spoonful onto an ungreased baking pan. Bake at 400 degrees for 15 minutes. Reduce temperature to 350 and bake until puffed up and golden brown, about 20–25 minutes more. Turn off the oven. Poke the bottom of each puff, turn upside down and let dry in oven for 10 minutes. Move to rack to cool.

Cream filling:

⅓ cup sugar	4 egg yolks
2 Tbsp. flour	1⅓ cups milk
2 Tbsp. cornstarch	¾ tsp. vanilla

Mix sugar, flour, cornstarch and egg yolks vigorously until mixture is thick. Simmer milk. Gradually add one-third of the hot milk into egg mixture. Stir to combine. Scrape egg mixture into pan and cook over low to medium heat, scraping so it doesn't burn. Cook mixture until it bubbles and custard is thick. Put custard in bowl and add vanilla. Cool. Spoon cooled custard into split puffs.

Dress-Up Gowns and High Heeled Shoes

While Marion was full of life in so many ways thanks to her gift for telling stories and bringing people together, there also lived in Marion a space that went unfulfilled. As marriage and motherhood brought her joy, it also brought responsibility that allowed for little else.

With the increasing responsibility of a home, husband, handicapped son, daughter and chicken farm, Marion's not-so-long-ago dancing days waltzed out the window leaving her dresses behind. Of course Marion would have liked more evenings to dance the night away with Clarence, but with more pressing priorities, dancing quickly became something of the past. In the end, although Marion no longer had use for her dancing dresses, fortunately, her daughter, Sharon, did.

As a young girl, Sharon had an absolute ball playing dress up in her mother's ballroom gowns that Hattie had sewn for Marion over the years. Sharon and her friend spent many hours dressing up in Marion's array of gowns, high heeled shoes, gloves and hats putting on quite the five year old fashion show. Thinking about those days, Sharon can't help but reflect on the bittersweetness Marion must have felt watching her daughter in pure bliss playing with the gowns she knew she would probably never wear again.

Women's Club

In the early forties, Marion joined the Women's Club, eventually becoming a fifty-year member. To honor her long-standing membership, the Club held a special ceremony where they presented several members with fifty-year pins. From that day on, Marion wore hers proudly on the lapel of her suit to each of the monthly meetings. The Women's Club was perfect for Marion. It was social and it was fun. Marion loved helping with the annual flower show, floats for the town parades and themed table setting event. One year, choosing a wedding theme, she went all out decorating her table using draped toile, china place settings, silver utensils and linen napkins. Like her baking, she did it up. Her other claim to fame was the float she designed and helped put together for Hollis's United States Bicentennial Parade in 1976. The float titled, "Women's Club Tea," had Marion dressed in her finest sitting around a table with several other elegant clubbers sipping tea on a moving, carpeted parlor. What the Women's Club did for Marion, Marion gave back.

Working Life

As earnestly as Marion liked to play, she and Clarence worked day and night to support their family just as their parents had done for them. Always thinking ahead, they began investing in their retirement early into their marriage because farmers were not covered under Social Security like other workers. Clarence and Marion needed to earn their own retirement. Every month, Clarence bought a twenty-five dollar savings bond for twelve dollars to save for their retirement. With money forever short, they saved first and spent second. Like their families before them, going into debt was not an option. Hattie, having lived a full life enjoying her grandchildren, died admirably with her last twenty dollars safely tucked in a drawer in her sewing machine.

In 1955, when Marion was forty-five, Stephen was twelve and Sharon was ten, she went back to work at the Lincoln

Store working forty hours a week making a dollar an hour. Her income was, in Sharon's words "enough to buy groceries, a few clothes and some odds and ends to appease mine and Stevie's teenage desires."

Marion's day started at dawn and ended about ten o'clock every night. Other than routine cooking, cleaning and ironing, she maintained a huge garden and took care of Stephen and Sharon. A typical morning schedule included cooking breakfast, packing lunches, getting the kids off to school, cleaning up the kitchen and milking equipment, washing a load of laundry, mixing up a cake and baking it, hanging the clean clothes on the clothesline, taking a bath, dressing for work and driving to work by 9:00 A.M.

After work, Marion came home to make supper, collect four to six gallons of milk from the milk cans to sell to the neighbors, clean up, finish the laundry and catch up on the bookkeeping.

Other than working, Marion and Clarence did enjoy having summer pond parties. In the late fifties they had a pond dug at the bottom of the field across the street where all the neighbors would come for a cookout. Clarence cooked hotdogs and hamburgers on a grill he rigged up near the pond and Marion always filled a basket with her homemade raisin cookies.

Florida Retirement

In 1974 Marion and Clarence tried on retirement for the first time. Buying an older motor home from Louis they drove to Fort Myers, Florida with Stephen to spend the winter and many thereafter. They loved being part of the retired farming community there. In Sharon's words, Marion was "in her element." It was very social. They played cards, shuffle board, bingo and oftentimes the ladies put on skits. One time Marion called Sharon from Florida to get some black cloth in the attic at Ranger Road so she could sew a bathing suit with matching lace-bordered pantaloons to wear in a last minute fashion show the ladies were putting on to raise money for something. Sharon was happy to see her mother having so much fun.

Fortunately, Clarence and Marion were able to enjoy fifteen winters in Florida before Clarence died in 1989 of prostate cancer. Clarence's death was a huge loss for Marion. Soon after he died, Sharon, in her thoughtful generosity, brought Marion and Stephen to Florida for a couple months to continue their winter tradition. Marion had made good friends in the trailer park that served her well after losing her husband.

Not to Be Outdone by Her Sister

As the years carried on Marion never lost her spunk. On her eighty-fifth birthday she celebrated by riding her neighbor's horse. Getting help up into the saddle, Marion proceeded to parade around her yard. Hilda arrived to wish Marion a happy birthday and not to be outdone by her younger sister figured if Marion could do it, so could she. So, sure enough, when Marion got off, Hilda got on.

For Marion's ninetieth birthday Sharon and Stephen had a party for her at the house. This time Marion rode her little red banana seat bicycle down the street. By her ninety-fifth birthday she didn't know what to ride until she realized that her nephew's motorcycle was in the garage. Although Marion probably would have liked to take it for a spin, she had more sense than that. Her family pulled it out for her to sit on and have her picture taken. It was perfect for her age. For her 100th birthday she planned ahead, thinking she would ride their John Deere sit-mower. Unfortunately, that day never came.

Marion, 1910–2006

In 1990 Sharon took Marion, Hilda and Hilda's daughter, Sue, on a little adventure to see Grandmother Lull's house in Grasmere. They knocked on the door of the white, block-like Georgian house hoping the owners would be kind enough to let them in. The owners graciously invited them inside to tour the house. Marion and Hilda thought much looked as it had when they lived there with Grandmother Lull seventy-five years before. It had the same big old windows, interior wooden shutters, high ceilings, tiny back stairway and large, square kitchen. Walking through the house, room by room, Marion and Hilda recalled sleeping in the expansive upstairs with no heat wondering why their family moved from one cold house to another. They shared memories of each and every space, particularly the room where they saw their deceased grandmother laid out on the table. That day had left quite an impression on six-year-old Marion. So much so that from that day on Marion did everything she could to avoid viewing the deceased or attending funerals.

Years later Marion let her adult children know her wishes regarding her own death. As Sharon recalled, "Mom made it clear to me and Stevie that when she died she didn't want a funeral or visiting hours or a memorial service. So, when mom died in December 2006, we didn't have a funeral. The night she died I sat up in bed with my yellow pad of paper to write my mother's obituary. I was mad about that because the night my father died we came home from the hospital and I helped mom write his obituary. It wasn't fun—we were all exhausted and I didn't want to have to do that again. I urged my mother to write her own obituary, but she never did. So, there I was again writing an obituary I had hoped I wouldn't have to. I had the last word, but I didn't want it.

I was frustrated so I listed mom's obituary under the name Ethel Marion Lull Howe instead of Marion Lull Howe, which is how people knew her. The girls around town told me, 'Sharon, we missed your mom's obituary.' I knew they had missed it because they didn't know her as Ethel.

Stephen and I decided to honor my mother's life by having a committal service at the Pine Hill Cemetery on what would have been my parent's sixty-seventh wedding anniversary, September 30, 2007. It was just me, Stephen, Hilda, Sue, and Sue's two daughters, Sarah and Anna. My husband Chip didn't even come. He never asked me about it so I left it alone. It was better that way. The service felt right—it was about my mother and the people who loved her most."

During one of my later visits with Sharon at Ranger Road I noticed a small framed poem done in needlework hanging on the wall that hadn't been there before. Sharon had bought the poem for herself on her own birthday because it reminded her of her mother. "My mother was a very upbeat, positive person. She did her best to always be cheerful and look on the bright side even though life had handed her many difficult times and misfortunes. This poem captures my mother's sentiment."

"Let your heart be light
Your cares be few,
And all of your wishes
Just might come true."

Marion (left) and Hilda, 1917

Marion (left) and Hilda, 2004

Hattie with her three grandchildren, 1946.
Stephen Howe, Sue Ellen Hildreth and Sharon Howe (seated).

Marion's 95th birthday on her nephew's motorcycle, 2005.
Sharon Howe and Stephen Howe standing.

CHAPTER 14

One to Another

Louis to Grace

From the time of Arthur's death in 1930, The Red Fruit Farm was owned equally by Louis, Hilda and Marion. About fifteen years later, soon after Louis and his wife, Grace, moved into their newly built house at 65 Broad Street, Clarence became concerned that should Louis run into financial trouble with the farm, his poultry business could be vulnerable to Louis's potential debt. Clarence could not afford to run that risk. He thought it would be best to have the farm exclusively in Louis's name, freeing Marion and Clarence from any financial liability tied to The Red Fruit Farm. Grace also encouraged her husband to become the sole owner of the farm given the benefits she saw, spoken or otherwise, of doing so. In particular, there had been vague discussions about possible tax benefits if Louis owned the farm independently.

Over the course of what must have been several discussions among Louis, Grace, Clarence, Marion, Hilda and Henry, the two sisters, whose names were on the farm's deed with Louis's, agreed to sign their portion of ownership over to their brother. Despite the fact that Marion and Hilda took pause in letting go of their share of the farm, they understood it as a necessary precaution to protect their assets. Regardless of ownership on paper, Marion and Hilda

fully trusted that Louis would honor his verbal agreement
with them, dividing the farm equally if they ever sold The
Red Fruit Farm. Years later, as sometimes happens, things
did not go according to plan.

Louis managed the farm until, in his sixties, his persist-
ent headaches from high blood pressure greatly impeded his
ability to meet the demands of farming. With each passing
day, as it became increasingly difficult for him to do what
needed to be done, he realized the time had come for him to
pass the work onto someone else. Louis approached Frank
Whittemore, who represented Brookdale, asking him if he
would be interested in leasing the land. He gladly took Louis
up on his offer.

In 1973, Louis suffered a stroke and Grace, feeling she
could not provide the care he needed, admitted him to a
nursing home. Assuming management of the farm, she continued the lease with Brookdale without interruption. Louis
lasted in the nursing home for five more years until he died
on November 30, 1978.

Upon Louis's death, Grace, as his surviving spouse,
became sole owner of The Red Fruit Farm. Grace's inheri-
tance consisted of twenty acres of land, thirteen of which
were apple orchards, an apple storage barn and her house at
65 Broad Street. Grace immediately assumed management
of the farm knowing full well that although she would never
farm it herself, she had every intention of protecting it.

Soon after Louis died, Frank Whittemore approached
Grace with an offer to buy Red Fruit Farm. Expecting she
would welcome the opportunity to free herself from the bur-
den of having a farm with no heirs to farm it, Frank was

surprised she had absolutely no interest in selling. But if you knew Grace then you would know she had her arms wrapped pretty snug around the farm. No one, no way, no how would change that for a long time. Nevertheless, Grace couldn't take care of the farm herself so she had to lease the land, sell it or let it go to ruin. In her eyes, leasing the land was the only viable choice. After declining Brookdale's offer to buy the farm, Grace hoped Frank would continue leasing the land. Mercifully, Frank did continue the lease, albeit reluctantly, until a young man named David Orde came into the picture.

Grace to David

In 1979, a year before graduating from the University of New Hampshire with a degree in plant science, David Orde started to plan ahead. He wanted to be a farmer. It was in his blood. Having grown up on his father's dairy farm in Hollis and working at Brookdale since the age of five he had all the preparation he needed to finally forge his own farming journey. He wanted to farm and he wanted to be his own boss.

Knowing Louis Lull had passed away, leaving Grace to manage the farm, David saw her situation as one with promising potential. So, he upped the ante, asking Grace if she would lease her land to him if he paid a higher price than Brookdale. Grace gave Brookdale an opportunity to meet David's price, but Frank, already feeling he was paying too much, declined; ending one partnership where another began.

David took over leasing the land from Grace with an informal understanding that future ownership might be a distant possibility. And it was that possibility that kept David working hard year after year. While he labored managing the farm, Grace took it upon herself to manage David.

Not long after David came onto the scene, Grace made the executive decision to change the name of the farm. It was 1980. What had been known as The Red Fruit Farm would now be Lull Farm. In this seemingly small gesture, Grace, like Louis years before, made a statement to the community. In hanging her own sign she was not only demonstrating her ownership of the farm, but also her commitment to it. David would have liked to have named the farm Winter Robin Farm after his bee keeping business, but he knew that would never happen. As part of his lease agreement with Grace, she held the naming rights. She didn't miss a needle in the haystack.

Grace and David's partnership would have been more than delicate had he not been accommodating to her whims. Her ability to influence others in her favor was impressive. David knew full well that his only real obligation to Grace was to pay her for leasing her land. But, as Grace would have it, she finagled a whole lot more out of the deal. David wasn't just the farmer of the land, he was also her house handyman, mailbox-to-door delivery man and errands man. He could have easily protested, but he didn't. His relationship with Grace was far more important than coveting his every ounce of pride. So, he swallowed his tongue and stuck around.

Grace was definitely the eminent warden of the farm and a frugal one at that. She oftentimes ran out of her house in her pajamas to make sure David wasn't wasting water as he cleaned the equipment after finishing a cider run. She didn't miss a trick. If the water for the cider press hadn't come from

David and Grace

her house via a pump hooked up in her basement, David might have had the luxury of being his own boss.

David persevered for five more years under his lease agreement with Grace until finally, in 1984, she agreed to sell him the farm; well, sort of. Grace wanted the sale to occur over a period of several years, perhaps to get used to the idea or maybe for some other unknown reason. Nevertheless, she cleverly constructed a Life Estate Agreement stipulating that David would pay her a minimum of $10,000 a year toward the $175,000 purchase price.

The only difference between the lease and the Life Estate was that it provided David with potential ownership of the farm at some unknown point in the future. In the meantime, Grace would retain full ownership of Lull Farm. As much as the arrangement was less than ideal, David could not pass it up. He had come too far to jeopardize what he hoped would be his future—Lull Farm.

David continued to pay his dues under this anything-but-idyllic arrangement for eleven long years until at last his perseverance finally paid off. In 1995, Grace transferred full ownership of Lull Farm to David Orde, with one relatively minor contingency—she could live in her house for the rest of her life. Upon her death the house would become his. As the new owner of Lull Farm, David gladly agreed.

David's Dog, Boone

Over the years Grace became quite attached to David's Coonhound-Black Lab, Boone, who she liked to say was half hers. She even wrote a short book about him that sold at Lull Farm. David got Boone while visiting one day at Sumner Spaulding's farm. He saw a little black puppy hobble out from under a parked tractor dragging one of its hind legs. David asked Sumner what had happened. He told him that a horse had stepped on the puppy's leg. Sumner was going to put the dog out of its misery. That's when David piped up saying he would take the dog. Poor Boone was a mess. He had a broken leg, a bad shoulder and worms. David brought Boone to the vet, putting him on the road to recovery.

Boone was the best dog David, or Grace, ever had. Whenever David was in the fields on the tractor Boone would run alongside him, back and forth, up and down each row following him. Years later, in Boone's old age when he could no longer run, Grace happily took care of him at her house. The day she tripped over him and broke her hip marked the beginning of the end for both of them.

Not long after Grace broke her hip, Boone did something he had never done before. He went right out to Route 122 where he got hit by a car and died. David thinks somehow Boone knew it was time for him to go, going out into the road like that because it was completely out of character for him. In all his years with Boone, he never strayed.

When Boone died, Grace asked David if he would please bury him behind her house which, in his usual generosity, he did. He buried Boone in the backyard next to the stone wall at a gravestone Grace had gotten for him inscribed, "1982–1998 Faithful & Beloved Friend." Grace adored Boone, but David never realized just how much until the day she asked him to have her own ashes buried next to Boone.

Three years later, David honored Grace's wish. She died in 2001 and doing as he had promised, he arranged to have her ashes buried next to his dog, with not even a gravestone.

Early in Louis's married life he had purchased two burial plots at the East Cemetery; one for him and one for Grace. He was buried there, though Grace obviously wasn't interested. She evidently preferred Boone over Louis.

After Grace

When Grace died she left her entire estate to the University of California at Santa Cruz to honor a deceased nephew on her side of the family who had attended there. Her estate was valued at $1,000,000. It consisted of accumulated savings from the farm, the sale of the farm, income from her teaching job and several investments.

So, that's how it went. Grace and Louis's combined estate went off to California while David assumed ownership of Grace's house, though he did have to pay Grace's executor for its contents, which had been appraised at $10,000. From one generation to the next, Lull Farm changed hands from Arthur to Louis to Grace and then to David, at which point the Lulls of Lull Farm would live on in name, but not ownership.

Arthur's Desk

After all was said and done—there was just one thing Marion hoped for. She wanted her father's mahogany secretary desk that Hattie had passed down to Louis. The desk had belonged to Arthur's father and Marion wanted very much to keep it in the family. She had fond memories of her father sitting at his desk doing his accounting and letter writing. Growing up she knew the contents of every little drawer and, in that knowing, she connected with her father. So, after Grace died Marion approached David to ask him if she could have the desk. In his accommodating way he of course wanted her to have the desk, but understandably asked her to pay him what he had paid for it.

Marion would never have been able to buy the desk had it not been for her dear friend who left her some unexpected money upon her death. When Marion received the gift of money in the mail, it was the first and only time Sharon ever saw her mother cry.

David's Lull Farm

David has been farming Lull Farm for over thirty years. In that time, it has grown to 250 acres of owned and leased land combined, of which about 170 acres are vegetables and eighty acres are fruit. His primary vegetable crop is sweet corn at eighty acres, followed by forty acres of pumpkins, ten acres of tomatoes, ten acres of beans, ten acres of squash and zucchini, four acres of potatoes, four acres of cabbage, two acres of lettuce, two acres of eggplant, two acres of peppers and the remaining six acres are various specialty vegetables. Fruits are grown on a total of just under eighty acres with fifty acres of apples, fifteen acres of peaches, seven acres of strawberries, three to four acres of blueberries and two acres of raspberries.

Although sweet corn continues to be Lull Farm's primary vegetable crop, on a per acre basis it is one of the least profitable due to its high production costs. But because it continues to be one of the most popular items, David responds by doing what's needed to keep a variety of sweet corn available to the community and beyond.

Supermarket Surge

Until the mid to late seventies, produce farming in New England was all about apples. From the fifties through the seventies farmers made a good living selling apples because only local farms supplied the grocery stores. Then, in the early eighties, when imports along with large domestic suppliers established themselves, the local apple market vanished. Prior to the infiltration of large suppliers and importers, grocery store produce throughout New England consisted of only apples and citrus. That was it. The citrus came from Florida and the apples came from New England. It was a time when farms did well selling apples wholesale to grocery stores, but for most farms, those days are gone.

Back in 1985, David sold 10,000 bushels of apples a year at $10 per bushel. He packed them in wooden crates to bring to Alexander's Market (now Hannafords). It was a simple process of pick, pack and deliver. Twenty-five years later, he sells substantially less and he has to fight for a ten dollar bill per bushel. It also requires more than picking, packing and delivering. Now, he has to pick, code each apple with a UPC sticker, package them in plastic bags and then deliver. The labor adds too much to his cost, making selling to grocery stores financially unfeasible. The only way for David to make a profit selling apples is to sell a variety and quality of apples that the stores don't have.

When grocery stores were just that—stores with groceries and nothing more—local farms thrived. Since then, as grocery stores have evolved into supermarkets, selling everything from pineapples to prescriptions and kiwis to q-tips, many local farms have, subsequently disappeared. In 1979, a grocery store in Salem, NH, boldly moved its produce section from the sidelines where it received no special attention to the front of the store. It was a phenomenal success. Food stores throughout New Hampshire and beyond soon followed suit. In an aim to give shoppers a farm-stand-feel in the produce section, supermarkets have established produce sections as large as or larger than most farm stores.

Since David had owned Lull Farm, the number of local farms in New England has greatly declined. Many farms have died as a result of not being able to compete with conglomerate suppliers such as Pacific Northwest that supply produce to large supermarket chains consisting of 150 stores or more. Food store chains operate major distribution centers that contract with mega farms (primarily in California) to supply their stores with produce all year long. This relationship between the supermarket chains and the few chosen mega farms satisfies the produce pipeline, in effect, weeding out the majority of local farms from the supermarket arena.

Supermarkets strive to be as centralized as possible to maximize their efficiency and cost savings. Prudent business that, at the same time, precludes supermarkets from dealing with numerous small scale farms to provide them with produce from January through December. As a result, the majority of smaller or local farms have become solely dependent on their local community to keep their doors open.

Farming in New England has completely changed from a wholesale to a retail market in response to the huge suppliers that have squeezed out local farms. Retail is the only way David can stay in business. As he says, "The slogan here is—wholesale is no sale."

Survival of the Fittest

David knows that Lull Farm's success depends on his and the staff's ability to make their retail operation exciting. They need to continually provide new specialty items that people have never seen or had before. In his words, "We have to constantly look for ways to be different and interesting by offering things that the supermarkets don't have."

David has always looked for ways to expand and diversify. In 1982, he rented the Jack Wood Farm, at the base of Merrill Lane, to put in four acres of strawberries to sell at the small farm stand there. He also planted the first acre of sweet corn, which at that time was enough. He has since added many more acres of sweet corn, strawberries and peaches in an effort to meet increasing demand. He also planted Lull

Farm's first pumpkins, tomatoes, green beans, potatoes, blue-berries and raspberries.

Surprisingly, Lull Farm crops bring in only forty percent of its total income. What David calls, the "controlled invest-ments" bring in most of the revenue. Controlled investments include the array of products that David buys from outside vendors to sell at the two Lull Farm Stands. These products include off-farm produce that he purchases from the Boston Market and non-produce items such as baked goods, cheese, milk, salad dressings and sauces as well as other specialty items. Seasonal products such as turkeys and Christmas trees also generate revenue.

The reselling that David does is somewhat reminiscent of what Arthur Lull and Harold Hardy had to do way back in the days when apples alone defined their farms. Even in the days when farms did well selling apples, it wasn't enough to support them through the winter. Fruit and vegetable farm-ers, like Arthur, Harold, and now David, had to find ways to generate money during the off season. Harold made his other half-living selling milk from the forty or so cows he had while Arthur had his ice business. David has controlled investments.

Niche Farming

Successful farming in New England means finding a niche. In other words, grow only what people want and only what the supermarkets don't have. David finds his niche by growing twenty-five varieties of potatoes, fifteen different types of hot peppers and thirteen varieties of eggplants. Coming up with produce that the supermarkets don't have has become all the more difficult. As food stores gain faster and further access to fruits and vegetables all over the world the notion of seasonal produce is quickly disappearing. David believes that in large part "People's desire factor is gone." Case in point, in the mid eighties Lull Farm made $30,000 from pick-your-own strawberries at a single location. Now, it brings in less than $20,000 at two locations. During the same era, Lull Farm sold lots of cut flowers, especially Easter lilies and Christmas poinsettias because grocery stores didn't have them. Now they do, so Lull Farm sells very few.

Weathering the Storm

Finding a farming niche isn't easy, but unfortunately this isn't the biggest challenge farmers, like David, face. Today their more critical concern is extreme weather conditions. The abundance of rain in particular brings several unexpected problems that David has to contend with every year. Most recently, it ruined David's pumpkin crop. He super-fertilized, he danced and he prayed, but he couldn't get the pumpkins to grow. He ended up buying a couple loads of pumpkins from Indiana and a few more loads from western Connecticut because he did not want Lull Farm or Halloween to look any different than it had in the past.

Another immediate problem from the rain has been the increasing number of gullies that David sees in the fields. The rain also makes apples susceptible to fungal disease, namely apple scab that leaves lesions on the apples and leaves, making them unacceptable for sale. Farmers try to prevent apple scab by spraying early in the season to contain spores.

The New Hampshire Department of Agriculture has long supported farmers throughout the state in an effort to both preserve and grow the industry. One example of this is the state's testing and trap setting program that is available to New Hampshire farmers free of charge. State consultants will set pheromone traps (a container baited with a chemical attractant or pheromone) every week during the corn growing season to catch moths that are known to completely destroy an entire field in a single night. In setting the traps the potential for moth damage is greatly lessened, which subsequently minimizes or can even eliminate the need for chemical spraying.

David also hires an independent fruit consultant to keep a watchful eye on the apple orchard from April through October. Coming to Lull Farm once a week, the consultant closely monitors the health of the apple buds, blossoms and maturing apples. As unhealthy plants don't flourish, David and farmers like him are vigilant about plant health from seed to fruit.

Maintaining plant health is difficult without minimal chemical spraying. As far as spraying is concerned, David says, "It's a big help. I could not farm successfully without it. Fortunately, the types and methods of spraying nowadays leaves minimal chemical residue on plants or fruit so it is much safer. Only ounces of chemicals are used per acre. It's not skull and crossbones like it used to be. It's all new chemistry now. It's stable. The chemicals don't translocate. Spraying is also highly regulated. Each time we spray we have to fill out a long New Hampshire Department of Agriculture form detailing the date we spray, the crop we spray, what we use, the active ingredients in the spray, how much we use and the weather conditions."

At the end of the year David completes a summary report detailing the quantities of each chemical used for each type of crop, as required by the New Hampshire Department of Agriculture. The Department imposes strict annual limits on all farming chemicals. To confirm compliance, random, unannounced on-site field inspections are done periodically throughout the year.

David is a farmer dedicated to the land. He does not like to spray but to keep plants healthy he sometimes has to. As he says, "It's pretty simple. I can't sell wormy corn or scabby apples." He believes that most farms in New England have no choice but to utilize minimal spraying to keep their crops healthy. Keeping plants healthy from seed to store requires constant attention.

Until I spent a few hours with David I never fully realized all that goes into fruits and vegetables. As much as I'd love to be a gardener, I'm not. I pride myself not on making things grow, but rather keeping the weeds at bay. If only the many perennial flowers that I've planted over the years grew as lush as the weeds, I'd have a yard of envy. For me, gardening is about beating the weeds. Until a few years ago we had weeds, some six feet tall, lining each side of our driveway. It was impressive. We have since had each side leveled and seeded with grass, but the fight continues. Every fall and spring I get out my favorite heavy duty clippers to cut back the encroaching greenery. It is at least a couple days of what I call gardening.

Organics

Organic farming in New England might not be realistic for the simple reason that keeping large crops healthy in today's weather is very difficult. Furthermore, smaller farms like Lull Farm cannot afford to operate two different systems—conventional and organic—simultaneously. In David's experience, the only way he sees organic being feasible in New England is on a very small scale where you sell to local restaurants and Farmers' Markets.

In David's view, "People need to get over 'organic' in a big way. The benefit of eating fruits and vegetables far outweighs the risk of any residue related problems. Agricultural chemicals are a very small slice of our chemical world. People might want organic, but what about the air we breathe or the cleaning products we use or the food additives and pharmaceuticals we ingest? If you have a rash on your skin you go to the doctor for treatment. I have to do the same thing with my produce."

As far as organic farming on a larger scale is concerned, David believes that organic operations warrant questioning. 'Organic' is such a broad term that it is difficult for consumers to know what they are getting when they buy organic. In a nutshell, "Feel great about eating fruits and vegetables. And by all means, wash them. Know your farmer and support your local farms all year long or there won't be any. It costs money to eat good food."

When I was last at my brother's in Amherst, Massachusetts, he had a small poster on his refrigerator titled, "Ten Good Reasons to Eat Locally Grown Food." It is put out by the Massachusetts Department of Agriculture in an effort to support local farms. In summary, it points out that:

1. Locally grown food tastes and looks better because it is fresh.

2. Locally grown food supports local farming.

3. Consumers know where their locally grown food is from.

4. Locally grown food builds a connection between farmer and consumer.

5. Locally grown food preserves open space.

6. Locally grown food keeps taxes down because most farms pay more in taxes than they usurp in town services.

7. Locally grown food helps sustain wildlife.

8. Locally grown food helps our planet's carbon footprint in that the food doesn't travel the average distance of 1,500 miles from farm to table.

9. Locally grown food supports life and land for future generations.

10. Locally grown food preserves genetic diversity. Where industrial agriculture strives to produce uniform produce with a long shelf life, resulting in just a few varieties within each fruit and vegetable category, local farms have the ability to grow many different varieties.[6]

We continue to learn more about the food we eat. With documentaries such as "King Corn" and "Food Inc.," in addition to the wide range of books available on the subject of food production, such as Omnivore's Dilemma or In Defense of Food by Michael Pollan, people are becoming increasingly aware of where their food comes from and how it is produced.

The Jamaicans

Hiring a strong work force is essential to the success of a farm. In 1984 Lull Farm and Kimball Farm were some of the first farms in the area to hire Jamaicans. David highly values the work of the Jamaicans whom he employs, because they know the work of farming. At home, they farm to eat and here they willingly work hard.

The process of hiring Jamaicans is regulated by the federal government. In January of each year, David completes a work order that he sends to an agent at the New England Apple Council requesting Jamaican workers for the upcoming season. David asks for the same workers from year to year by indicating their assigned J numbers on each work order. Each season the hourly wage is set by the government (currently $9.50 per hour).

Farm owners are not permitted to hire any foreign employees unless open job requisitions listed with the federal unemployment office go unfilled by domestic or local applicants. Every year before David completes his work order the vacancies must first be posted with the unemployment office. In David's experience no one ever applies, giving him the green light to go ahead and hire Jamaicans. With the recent downturn in the economy David expected local applicants. Much to his dismay, no one applied. He surmises that the lack of interest might be due to the intensity of the work.

When the Jamaicans first came to work at Lull Farm they lived in Nashua during the harvesting season. Since 1985, they have lived above the Lull Farm Stand in Hollis. David usually hires eight Jamaicans over the course of the busy season. He hires three in April, two in May and three more in

June. As the season winds down, the Jamaicans return home. Five or six go home in November and the other two or three go home in mid December.

David has a great relationship with the Jamaicans who work with him. They are hard workers and he admires them for that. They work together harvesting the land, making a living doing it. In large part it is who they each are and in that, they connect.

> *My kids and I have made it a tradition to carve pumpkins at Lull Farm the day before Halloween. The Jamaicans run quite the pumpkin carving camp a few days leading up to Halloween. They carve piles of pumpkins with such artistry that it's contagious. And better than that, they love company. So we, along with other die-hard carvers of all ages, grab a pumpkin or two or three to add to the cast of pumpkin characters. The long-bed trailer, carving tools and, above all, Jamaican energy make for an hour or two well spent. On Halloween night we return to Lull's to feast our eyes on the pumpkin exhibit extraordinaire.*

Perseverance

About eight years ago a national farming consultant from the 1st Pioneers Farm Credit Union, which lends money to New Hampshire farmers, advised David "to stop farming before you go out of business." The consultant knew as well as David that agriculture was spiraling downward. Twenty years ago there were more than fifteen commercial fruit farms in New Hampshire. Now there are no more than a few.

Although David understands why farms, both large and small, have been dwindling for a long time, he has no intention of going out of business. In fact, he is all the more motivated to do whatever he can to help keep farming alive. But, with all its difficulty, why? "I do it because it allows me to work for myself. I also like to watch things grow. I get satisfaction from seeing the process of nothing turn to something, when the first leaf unfolds to when you start harvesting. I'm not going to get rich farming, but I do make a living. Financially, farming is a bobbing effect where you do fine for a bit and then you grab a gulp of air hoping to resurface. Between the rising cost of labor, equipment, fertilizer and property taxes, I need to make steady sales all year long to stay afloat."

The truth is, David can't imagine doing anything else. He farms like his father farmed and his grandfather farmed. It is what he knows and he has chosen it. With all its toil and tribulation, farming brings a unique sense of accomplishment. He gives to land and the land gives back.

Looking Ahead

In David's commitment to stay in business, the question he constantly faces is—how? Above all, he knows he cannot sit still. He has to keep new things coming all the time, which means planning ahead. Back in 1995 David invested in 100 acres of what was once a dairy farm in Milford, to raise beef cattle. He wants to establish a small meat business under the Lull Farm umbrella. He is in the process of accumulating a herd of registered Herefords from which he will sell local hay raised beef at the two Lull Farm Stands, one in Hollis and the other in Milford. With hay raised beef on the horizon he will also be raising chickens to sell quality roasters and broilers that, like the beef, are not available at local stores.

As always, David will continue to work on expanding Lull Farm's fruit and vegetable selection. Next on his list are radishes and beets. Other than these projects he doesn't know what the future brings. He does know, however, that whatever he does, he won't sit still.

Looking Back

Behind the registers at the farm stand in Hollis there is a photograph of David as a six-year-old boy, standing under a large apple tree in full blossom on Lull Farm. It was taken by Hilda. Who would have guessed back then that the six-year-old boy standing under the apple tree would one day become the owner of the farm he was standing on? David is carrying on what began many years ago as selling apples and cutting ice. He is making a living on his own watch, keeping a farm alive. As he says, "I'm not going anywhere. I'm gonna die with my boots on."

Life of the Land

After Marion died, Sharon inherited her parents' farmland on Ranger Road with no farmer to farm it. Knowing that a farm without a farmer can often lead to its demise she hopes, like Grace, she can keep it alive. Grace could have easily sold the land, which would have likely led to development, but she did not. And that's a good thing because what was a farm is still a farm.

Sharon hopes she too can do as Grace did. Thanks to David, her husband, Chip, and Brookdale, who is growing crops in one field, the farm has endured. Sharon and her brother, Stephen, could have easily taken the road more traveled, selling the land, but they have chosen not to because they know that once they do, their land will in all probability never be farmed again.

Full Circle

After Clarence died in 1989, Sharon's husband, Chip Harris, took over haying the fields on Ranger Road. After years of doing it Chip is ready to pass the torch. He and Sharon asked David if he would be interested in haying. David, in need of hay for his stock of Herefords, said he would. Sharon and Chip told David they would sell him the hay for twenty-five cents per bale. David, paying twice that amount for other hay, generously offered to pay Sharon and Chip fifty cents per bale.

David and his son, Andrew, hay the Ranger Road fields twice a year—at the end of May and the end of August. This past year they cut 2000 bales, making it a productive venture for all involved.

What started in 1918 as apples and ice has found itself reconnected by way of hay, generations later. The people have changed, but the land has endured.

I recently learned that David Orde grew up in the same house as Marion. David's grandparents, Al and Beryl Orde, moved into 60 Broad Street after buying the north side of the farm from Hattie when she sold it soon after the hurricane. Al and Beryl had two children Al and Mary Ellen. Years later young Al married a woman named Marion. They moved into the small ell of the house toward Wheeler Road where they brought up their three children, David, Douglas and Deborah. Douglas runs Hollis Construction and Deborah manages the Lull Farm Stand in Milford.

David grew up in the same house where the Lulls put their mattresses on the kitchen floor to fall asleep after arriving from New Boston. As a boy, he played in the same barn where Marion split open shell beans on the floor. He played in the same pasture where Marion would walk the cows with Althea. He sat in the same front room where Arthur and Louis stayed up late listening to the radio. He turned on the same light switch that for the Lulls was a first. Where the Ordes' cows roamed, the Lulls' cows roamed. David's father and grandfather farmed, just as Marion's father and grandfather farmed. So, at this very juncture, there is, as always, more than meets the eye. The land lives through generations, passing, as do our stories, from one to another.

Reflection

Through the process of writing this book I often asked myself, why had I taken on such a task? The prevailing answer I have come to realize only through finishing is that I met Marion when she opened her door wide when another door in my life was closing. My mother was diagnosed with Alzheimer's disease in 1996. Over the next six years I watched her go. It was a long, unfinished goodbye. My mother died in 2002 in a nursing home with me and my brothers at her side. And although we did say goodbye to her, the woman lying in that bed was not the mother we knew or remember.

I think I stuck with this book because in hearing Marion's stories and then Sharon's and then Hilda's, I connected with them, but even moreso, with my mother. Their stories reminded me of some of my own, which through writing I connected to my mother in a way that Alzheimer's did not allow. I persevered in finishing because doing so brings closure to my relationship with Marion and more than that, with my mother. In the end, as Marion kept her father's eyeglasses and I kept my father's scrapbook, I now "Hold onto this book."

Special Thanks

I could not have done this without the consistent help of Sharon Howe who picked up where Marion left off. Sharon told me many of the stories in this book and provided most of the photographs. She also read several drafts, meticulously editing each one. I thank Hilda Hildreth for her stories, typing, clarifications and photographs. I also thank Sue Birch for her additions and editing. Thank you to David Orde for giving me a crash course in agriculture and more than that, telling me his story of Lull Farm. I would also like to thank Audrey Augun who cheered me on, giving me the thumbs up to keep going, when I needed it most. To Dana O'Shea, thank you for bringing fresh eyes and reinforcement to what had become many blurry pages. Thank you to Steve Macintosh for his support and spot-on suggestions. To Lea Gardner-Elkin, thank you for recognizing and encouraging the writer in me. I could not have done this without you. I also thank Bruce Goss for his encouragement. Thank you to Pattie Beckett and Lorna Condon for their support. And thank you to Norma Woods who gave me a poignant boost of confidence at the start. I also thank Puritan Press for their help.

To my children, Garlande, John and Christopher, thank you for your patience when I was invisible with my laptop and thank you for your help. To my husband, Bob, I thank you with all my heart.

Sources

Photographs

Photographs have been copied and included with permission by Sharon Howe, Hilda Lull Hildreth, Sue Birch, or David Orde.

Endnotes

1. PDS: The Planetary Data System, "Welcome to the Planets," NASA, http://pds.jpl.nasa.gov/planets/captions /smallbod/hal1910.htm.

2. The pre-1975 data are the Consumer Price Index statistics from *Historical Statistics of the United States* (USGPO, 1975). All data since then are from the annual *Statistical Abstracts of the United States* (U.S. Census Bureau).

3. *Oxford Pocket American Dictionary of Current English* (New York: Oxford University Press, 1999), p. 7.

4. New Hampshire Historical Society, www.nhhistory.org.

5. How Products are Made, Volume 5, "Eggs," http://www.madehow.com/Volume-5/Eggs.html.

6. Massachusetts Deparatment of Agricultural Resources, "Fresh from the Farm: The Massachusetts Farm to School Cookbook," State of Massachusetts, http://www.mass.gov/agr /markets/Farm_to_school/farm_to_school_cookbook.pdf.